The River Cottage

Cakes Handbook

The River Cottage Cakes Handbook

by Pam Corbin

introduced by
Hugh Fearnley-Whittingstall

www.rivercottage.net

BLOOMSBURY
LONDON · BERLIN · NEW YORK · SYDNEY

In memory of lovely Philippa

First published in Great Britain 2011

Text copyright © 2011 by Pam Corbin
Photography © 2011 by Gavin Kingcome

The moral right of the author has been asserted

Bloomsbury Publishing Plc, 36 Soho Square, London W1D 3QY
Bloomsbury Publishing, London, New York and Berlin

A CIP catalogue record for this book is available from the British Library

ISBN 978 1 4088 0859 7

10 9 8 7 6 5 4 3 2 1

Project editor: Janet Illsley
Designer: Will Webb
Photographer: Gavin Kingcome

Printed and bound in Italy by Graphicom

www.bloomsbury.com/rivercottage

Contents

You may already know of Pam Corbin through her wonderful *River Cottage Preserves Handbook*, or perhaps you have attended one of her preserving courses down here at Park Farm. Her expertise relating to jams, jellies, chutneys, cordials and liqueurs is unsurpassed, and her down-to-earth way of sharing that knowledge has made her one of the most popular members of our team. That's why, when Pam agreed to channel her considerable talents into a book dedicated to cake, I was filled with pleasure and, indeed, greedy anticipation. You won't be surprised to hear that I stepped up to my professional responsibilities and made myself available for sampling as the book progressed. It was a tough job… Now, having read the book, cooked a number of the recipes for my family at home, and eaten many others hot from Pam's tins (or picked up from my special cake sample drop box at River Cottage HQ), I would venture to say that this may be the only cake-baking book you'll ever really need.

What I love about Pam is that she's a champion of the art of the possible. Having proved that there is nothing mysterious or arcane about the art of preserving, and that fabulous preserves are within the reach of any cook, Pam has performed a similar magic on the subject of baking. While many of us enjoy whipping up a batch of muffins or a chocolate sponge – and many more need very little encouragement to sample the results – a lot of cooks are under the misapprehension that they're not great cake-makers, or somehow lack the special touch needed to produce great results. If that strikes a chord with you, then this book should set you right. Not only is it an invitation to rediscover an enormous range of delectable cakes and biscuits, it's also a confidence-inspiring demonstration that we can all create them if we want to.

There are literally thousands of different cakes, bakes, scones, biscuits and cookies that Pam might have chosen to showcase here, but I think there's something rather brilliant about the range she has selected. She's combined a raft of wonderfully nostalgic regional recipes, such as Cornish fairings, Grasmere gingerbread and Dundee cake, with some intriguing and often rather sophisticated options, such as Italian certosino or her delicate little marzipan-filled Simnel cakelets. There are a few surprises – I absolutely love Pam's 'Veg patch' gnome cakes and her homemade Jammy dodgers. But all the recipes are based on the principles we try to stick to at River Cottage: many focus on seasonal ingredients, several use up leftovers and, of course, Pam encourages us to make use of local produce, including herbs and fruit we might have growing in our own gardens.

You won't find elaborately decorated cakes here, or swathes of fondant icing and sugarpaste – and thank goodness, I would say. Pam never goes down the route of novelty for novelty's sake, which is very liberating for the cook. Who wants to worry about piping and moulding when there's cake to be eaten? And it doesn't mean these cakes and bakes aren't beautiful to look at. As Pam says, she simply believes in allowing a cake's natural charms to speak for themselves. The result is that while Pam's cakes always look stunning to me, there's nothing here that doesn't taste at least as good as it looks…

It's got to be said – and I think this is very sad – that cake has rather fallen out of favour in some quarters. It can be seen as an over-indulgent foodstuff without nutritional value. But, with the best homemade cakes, that's just not fair. While I'm not suggesting we should all be cramming ourselves with macaroons and Battenberg every day, I think sweet baked treats have an important part to play in a well-balanced, life-enhancing diet. There are cakes for special occasions, of course – the birthday cakes and Christmas tree biscuits, or Pam's elegant pudding cakes such as the Seville orange polenta cake – but plenty of others which fulfil a more everyday need. A slab of fruity 'Elevenses' lumberjack cake, a slice of Banana bread or a chunk of Pam's lovely 'Bird table' bread cake are all fantastic ways to fill a hungry gap between breakfast and lunch, or to fuel yourself on a long walk. And Pam packs so many of her cakes with fruit, seeds and vegetables, as well as the obvious eggs, milk and flour, that she demonstrates time and again that cake can be a sustaining, wholesome option, not just 'empty calories'.

Pam also has an eye on the clock. She understands that, while it's lovely to spend an entire afternoon ensconced in the kitchen, turning out Swiss rolls, tray bakes and buns, it's not always possible. Consequently, there are plenty of cakes here, including the divine Banana and chocolate cake as well as the classic Victoria sandwich, which you could have on the table, warm and irresistible, within the hour. And I also love the fact that many of these cakes are great 'keepers': invest a little time in mixing and baking them, and they'll sit happily in a cake tin for days, even weeks – in a few cases, months – improving all the while.

This book, then, is much more than a collection of scrumptious treats to be enjoyed once in a while. It's a comprehensive call for the revival of cake, in all its many glorious guises. It's a celebration of home-baking with good, well-sourced ingredients, an argument for the revival of elevenses and four o'clock tea, an acknowledgement of the simple pleasure of offering a cuppa and a slice of something nice to someone you care about. You may be a seasoned baker with a string of village-show rosettes to your name – in which case, you will find plenty here to expand your repertoire, and probably garner a few more gongs! But even if you are a novice who has only dabbled on the shores of flapjacks and fairy cakes, I urge you to feast your eyes on Pam's work. These carefully crafted, inspiring and utterly delicious recipes will bring out the baker in you, I promise.

Hugh Fearnley-Whittingstall, East Devon, January 2011

Getting Started

Mention the word cake and it seems to touch the heart and find the soul – communicated in a mistiness of the eyes and an affirming whisper of '*I love cake*'. These days, in this world of cup-cake cornucopia, the weekly baking day has been almost swept away amidst the candy-coloured, swirly-topped cakes that are so freely available from countless retail outfits. Now, I don't want you to think I'm a spoilsport, and I'll be the first to admit the chance of a coffee, slice of cake and a chat is always high on my list of priorities. But what could be more pleasurable, or time better spent, than an hour or two of baking in the kitchen, radio on, with cake fumes airily wafting into every corner of the house? What better gift can we hand down to our children than the skill to take natural ingredients and turn them into something to nourish and sustain; and more often than not in the case of the cake, make something special to mark and celebrate an important occasion?

My mum made cakes and so did her mum. Baking day generally fell on Friday, ensuring that there was always cake in the tin for the weekend, especially for tea on Sunday. These treasured bakes were offered only when the bread and butter – or come to that, anything else vaguely filling – had been eaten up. This was the moment that the cake was cut. After that, the supplies in the cake tin were rationed to last the rest of the week, although sometimes, thankfully, there was a midweek boost of freshly made flapjacks. As a consequence, the cake tin itself prompted rushes of pleasure or disappointment with a '*thank goodness*' when reassuringly heavy, or '*oh bother*' when light and empty.

I can't remember a time when I didn't make cakes and I have certainly never considered baking in the slightest way a chore. You don't have to be extraordinarily talented or have heaps of time to make cakes. A simple baking session requires a few store-cupboard ingredients, plus a little of your time. From mixing to devouring, a panful of muffins can be ready within 30 minutes and the quintessential and much-loved Victoria sandwich doesn't take much longer. Of course, it makes economic sense, too. Not only will the cost of these home-baked goodies be a fraction of their commercial counterparts, your sense of fulfilment will be priceless. And those lucky enough to be nurtured by cake will keep the memories of your baking long into old age; a good cake lingers in the memory long after the last crumb has been eaten.

The history of cake goes back a long way, its evolution spanning thousands of years. It would appear our Neolithic ancestors made cakes in some form or another, but these early attempts were a far cry from our notion of a cake. Their cakes were flat and hard, made from little more than a mix of moistened crushed grain and baked on a hot stone – an early prototype of our oatcakes today. Since then, cakes as we know them have evolved bit by bit. The ancient Egyptians added honey, while the Romans included raisins, nuts and fruit.

Sweet spices, eggs and sugar were incorporated into recipes during the sixteenth century and records show that yeast was used to leaven these lavishly enriched cakes. By the beginning of the eighteenth century, cakes were beginning to be made without yeast. Instead, eggs were whisked for up to an hour until they were light and voluminous. As a consequence, dutiful cooks, who were keen to ensure their cakes rose, ended up with 'wrestler's wrists'. Mercifully, during the 1840s, Alfred Bird (who, incidentally, also devised custard powder) created a mix of bicarbonate of soda (alkaline) and cream of tartar (acid) and formed what has become known as modern-day baking powder. After that, and with the help of more easily regulated ovens, cake-making became more or less… a piece of cake.

Even the shortage of food, along with its strict rationing, during the war did not stop cake-making. While land girls dug for victory by growing vegetables, determined housewives improvised and made frugal cakes without eggs – using carrots or potatoes and whatever sort of fat was available.

Bearing in mind the enforced parsimony of those adverse times, baking with the wealth of fabulous ingredients we can tap into these days has never been quite so easy or universally accessible. From simple-to-make daily treats to those gorgeous goodies we dream about, take pleasure in your baking – it's a lifetime skill, which will only get better.

Baking gear

Cake-making isn't a dressy affair – just swap your kid gloves for oven gloves and wear an apron and comfy clothes (heels are optional). However, if you are going to get serious about cake-making (and I hope you do), investing in a few pieces of useful equipment will certainly make it easier and more satisfying. When a cake pops out of its tin perfect, whole and undamaged, it's a real moment of joy.

You'll be able to find all the items I mention here in a well-stocked kitchen shop (which will also be a pleasure to browse around), or from various internet sources. It's always advisable to buy the best quality you can afford: top-notch items, chosen with care, will become reliable kitchen aids that last a lifetime. But there is no need to go into debt to keep the family in cakes. The chances are, you'll already have most of the things you need – and too much stuff will clutter up the kitchen drawers.

Electric mixer

Buying a simple hand-held electric whisk is a shrewd move: it will save you time and elbow grease. Many recipes require butter and sugar to be beaten together until 'very light and creamy'. By hand, with a wooden spoon, it can take 10–15 minutes to get to this stage. With a hand-held whisk, it can be reached in about 5 minutes. A free-standing electric mixer is a real boon for creaming, whisking and rubbing-in methods. A food-processing attachment or a separate machine is useful for processing nuts, etc. But these large bits of equipment are expensive and, in general, all cake-mixing processes can be undertaken by hand or with a hand-held electric whisk.

Mixing bowls

A selection of different-sized mixing bowls is helpful. The roomy proportions of good old-fashioned earthenware basins are excellent for most cake-making methods and the bowls are sufficiently heavy to sit firmly on the work surface without moving whilst ingredients are being mixed together. A 30–32cm bowl will be adequate for most average cake mixes. Do keep a lookout in charity shops and market stalls for vintage mixing bowls, a lovely addition to your kitchen.

Scales

A good set of scales is essential. Good results rely on accurate measuring. Flat-bed digital scales are handy to weigh ingredients straight into the mixing bowl.

Wooden spoons

These are useful for beating, mixing and stirring, as they do not scratch non-stick surfaces or conduct heat. The unsealed wood can hold strong flavours, such as garlic and spices, so it is worth dedicating one or two spoons to cake-making alone.

Metal spoons

Large metal spoons are best for folding a lighter or drier mixture into a heavy one.

Measuring spoons

A set of graded measuring spoons, from ¼ tsp/1.25ml to 1 tbsp/15ml, will give you the exact spoon quantities necessary for successful baking.

Measuring jug

An angled jug that can be read from above is useful for measuring liquid ingredients, particularly for recipes such as muffins that use several liquids.

Spatula

A spatula or 'scraper' with a flexible head is helpful for folding in, as well as scraping out the mixing bowl so that all the cake mix gets into the baking tin.

Sieve

A fine-meshed sieve is essential for aerating compacted flour and icing sugar. It is worthwhile having a couple of sieves, one for dry ingredients and one for wet. A good sharp tap over the kitchen sink will remove any residual floury grains from the mesh of your 'dry' sieve and will save you having to wash it.

Citrus zester or fine grater

This will enable you to easily remove the highly flavoured and aromatic zest from citrus fruit without the bitter pith underneath.

Wire cooling racks

These footed metal grid racks allow air to circulate around cakes so they can cool more quickly. You'll need at least two to enable you to turn a cake out of its baking tin, then straight away re-invert it onto a second rack. This double action helps to prevent criss-cross grid markings on the top of the cake. Cooling racks are usually either rectangular or round. Look out for tiered racks that fold away, which are a tremendous aid for a big baking session or a kitchen short of space.

Oven thermometer

An inexpensive but good oven thermometer is well worth investing in, so you can check how accurate your oven temperature is. If you discover the temperature of your oven is not what it says on the dial (a not uncommon occurrence), the thermometer will help you achieve the correct temperature for each recipe.

Baking tins

For good results, it is essential to use the right-size tin for a recipe. However, this doesn't mean you have to use a round (or square) tin if that's what the recipe says. A 20cm round tin is roughly the same as an 18cm square one. Keep in mind the volume of a square tin is about the same as a round tin that is 2cm bigger.

Loose-bottomed tins are ideal for easily turning out cakes that won't come to any harm if inverted, such as the two halves of a Victoria sponge. But cakes with delicate or streusel-type toppings are best baked in a clip-sided springform cake tin. The following assortment should be sufficient for most baking requirements:

2 x 20cm sandwich tins
1 x 23cm springform tin (with spring-release clip on the side for easy release)
1 x 23cm garland or ring mould (circular, with a hollowed-out centre)
1 x 1 litre loaf tin (about 20 x 10cm)
1 x 2 litre loaf tin (about 25 x 13cm)
1 x 30cm x 20cm Swiss roll tin
1 x 18cm square tin
1 x 12-hole muffin tray
1 x 12-hole fairy cake tin
1 or 2 large baking sheets (for biscuits)

Good baking tins can be pricey but they are a sound investment and should last a lifetime. My favourite tins are made by Alan Silverwood Ltd (see directory, p.244).

Manufactured in the UK, the light anodised alloy conducts heat evenly and speedily and you may well find baking times can be reduced a little. The tins also release their cakes easily. The range includes a good choice of shapes and sizes, including an ingenious multi-size tin and a special Battenberg tin. Although the tins are not dishwasher safe, the smooth surfaces are very easy to clean with hot soapy water.

Otherwise, go for good heavy-duty, non-stick bakeware, such as the Masterclass range from Kitchen Craft (see directory, p.244), available from most good cookshops, or the Cook and Bake range from Lakeland (see directory, p.244). Much as I've tried, I seem to have little success with silicone baking moulds, usually ending up with a crumby-looking cake plus the laborious job of cleaning out the mould. But perhaps it's me, and somewhere along the line I've got it wrong.

Lining and baking papers

Used to line tins, these prevent cakes sticking. The various options are as follows:

Greaseproof paper This needs to be lightly greased before using to line baking tins. It's also ideal for wrapping cakes and biscuits to be stored in an airtight container.

Baking parchment A silicone-coated non-stick paper, this is easy to use and effective; there's no need to grease it. Look out for unbleached baking parchment. You can keep the baking parchment used for rolling out biscuits, etc. Just wipe over, roll up and keep till next time.

Bake-O-Glide The satin of the baking world. A Teflon-coated non-stick fabric, it can be reused hundreds of times. Although it may seem a bit costly, a moderate-sized roll will kit out your favourite baking tins in silky smooth underwear that will have your cakes slipping out of their corset-like armoury quite effortlessly. The downside is that it's not biodegradable – but of course this is offset by the fact that you are not using hundreds of pieces of baking parchment.

Baking parchment cake-tin liners Shaped to fit neatly into specific sizes of baking tins, these quick-release liners withstand oven temperatures up to 230°C/Gas mark 8. They are particularly time-saving if you are batch-baking.

Muffin, cup cake or fairy cake papers These are ideal for making small yet perfectly formed cakes. Use them singly to line the cups of muffin or cup cake trays, or tripled if you want them to stand free on a baking tray.

Edible wafer paper Made from potato or rice starch, this is used to line baking trays and helps light, sugary bakes like macaroons hold together and release easily.

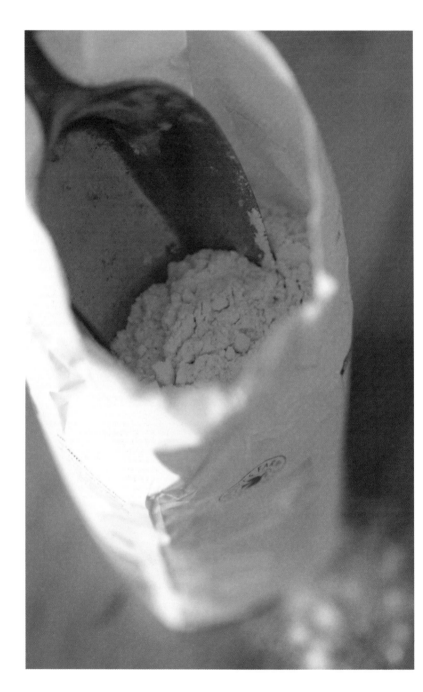

Cake ingredients

From quick-to-make homely griddle cakes to fabulous, light and billowy egg-blown sponges, the vast majority of cakes are made from four store-cupboard ingredients: flour, eggs, sugar and fat (usually butter). It's quite incredible how varied cakes can be, considering the basic elements most of them have in common – but of course, ever since humankind has been baking, we've been using a few extra choice ingredients to work small but crucial changes. Dried fruit, spices, nuts, coconut, fresh fruit, vegetables, honey, treacle and coffee all spring to mind, as well as the temptress Ixcacao, the goddess of chocolate. These added ingredients can transform a plain cake into anything from a hearty family filler to a gâteau to die for.

One of the greatest advantages of home-baking is that it gives us choice. Home cooks have control over their own ingredients and we can choose local, sustainable, organic or fairly traded options if we want to. A cake won't go horribly wrong if you don't use free-range eggs or fair-trade bananas, but I always keep in mind the saying, 'What you put in, is what you take out'. I think that's true on many levels, not just in terms of simple flavour. Remember, too, that your time is precious: you owe it to yourself to use good ingredients because they add untold value to your baking.

Before you get going, it's well worth taking a little time to learn how ingredients work together, so that every cake you bake will be a triumph. I'll start with the key players, the ones that combine to form the foundation of most cakes.

Flour

Flour is the backbone of a cake. Cakes can be made without eggs, sugar and fat, but rarely are they made without some sort of flour. Cake flours are generally sold as either 'plain' flour, without raising agents, or 'self-raising', which has the correct ratio of raising agent added. Plain flour is ideal for biscuits, fruit cakes, gingerbread and fine-textured cakes that rely on tiny air bubbles trapped in beaten egg to give lift. Self-raising flour is very handy for quick-mix batter cakes where the recipe does not rely on creaming or whisking to incorporate air into the mix. All flour needs to be sifted, sometimes twice, to aerate it and free up any compacted particles. If you sift wholemeal flour, don't throw away the husky bits left in the sieve. Re-combine them with the sifted flour – it's the goodness of the whole grain you are after.

Wheat flour This baking staple introduces protein, in the form of gluten, to a cake, and it's this gluten that gives a cake its structure, allowing the crumb to stretch and expand as the cake bakes, then 'holding' the risen shape. Wheat is graded into three different strengths, depending on the quantity and type of gluten it contains: finely textured 'soft' flour is best for cakes; 'hard' or 'strong' flour is best for bread-making; very hard durum wheat flour is used for pasta.

Wheat flour is available as white or wholemeal. Wholemeal is milled from the entire wheat grain, whereas white flour is milled from grains with the nutrient-rich bran and wheatgerm removed. Although white flour is used more often than not for cake-making, wholemeal flour can replace it partially, or completely, in most recipes. The coarser texture of wholemeal flour may give a slightly more dense texture to a cake – but sometimes that's just what we want!

If you like to use a mix of white and wholemeal flour, it's useful to keep a dedicated container of half-and-half mix for easy weighing out. Always check the best-before date as the higher concentration of oils in wholemeal flour can cause it to go rancid relatively quickly. Store all flours in sealed containers and keep in a cool, dark and dry place.

There are many different brands of wheat flour to choose from. I favour those which are neither bleached nor over-processed. My favourite flours come from Doves Farm and Marriage's (see directory, p.244); both can be sourced from most health food shops and some supermarkets.

Non-wheat flour

Non-wheat flours, such as rice, corn, polenta, potato and chestnut, can be used in conjunction with wheat flour to add specific flavours and textures to a cake. With the exception of spelt, they contain no gluten, so you can use them on their own if you need to exclude wheat from your diet. However, the results will be different – a little denser or heavier, but still delicious.

Spelt A distant cousin of wheat, spelt produces a deep nutty well-flavoured flour. Although it contains gluten, the structure is rather more delicate and brittle than the gluten in wheat flour and it is more easily absorbed by the body. Sharpham Park (see directory, p.244) produces excellent spelt flour from UK-grown spelt.

Cornflour Milled from the heart of the maize kernel, cornflour is very fine and powdery. It does not contain any gluten and is rarely used in cake-making. However, when combined with wheat flour, it makes extraordinarily good shortbread.

Rice flour Produced from either white or brown rice, this is often used in gluten-free recipes, in combination with other ingredients such as ground almonds, coconut or grated vegetables.

Polenta This is produced from ground maize kernels and is therefore gluten-free. It is rich yellow in colour and is either fine- or coarse-ground. Fine-ground polenta is generally used for baking and is sometimes combined with ground almonds to produce a slightly grainy, yet moist cake.

Potato starch flour This is made by grinding potatoes to a pulp, removing the starch and then drying it until it can be ground into a powder. Potato starch is gluten-free and often used as one of the ingredients in pre-mixed gluten-free cake flours.

Oats Rich in protein and fibre, and with a lovely nutty flavour, oats are the main ingredient in flapjacks and muesli-type bars. More often than not, rolled (porridge) oats are used, but some recipes, such as parkin, call for oatmeal or oat flour.

Chestnut flour High in carbohydrate and starch, chestnuts contain no gluten or cholesterol and can be ground to a glorious, nutty-sweet flour to be used in special cakes and biscuits.

Gluten-free and wheat-free flours Excellent gluten-free cake flours, blended from a mix of non-wheat cereals with added raising agents, such as cream of tartar and bicarbonate of soda, are available from Doves Farm and Bia Nua (see directory, p.244). These flours also usually contain xanthan gum – a natural substance derived from corn syrup, which is often employed as a substitute for gluten because it improves crumb structure. You can buy it in most health food shops. Made with Bia Nua's gluten-free cake flour, my Victoria sandwich works a treat.

Raising agents

Some cakes rely wholly on the actual method used to make them rise, i.e. the whisked method, whereas others make use of raising agents. Baking powder is a mix of alkaline and acidic substances (bicarbonate of soda and cream of tartar respectively). When combined in the presence of moisture, they release gas which forms thousands of tiny bubbles and inflates the cake batter. This instant reaction is why, traditionally, it has always been important to get a cake mix into the tin and into the oven as soon as possible after adding liquid. However, these days, most modern baking powders are described as 'double action' and require heat as well as moisture for the real rise in the cake, giving the cook a bit more time. Bicarbonate of soda can be used on its own as a raising agent, but only works if there is acidity present from other ingredients. Yoghurt, buttermilk, apples, citrus fruit, cocoa, honey and treacle are all acidic and will give the necessary reaction when combined with bicarb.

Always measure raising agents precisely, so for 1 level tsp, level the measure off with the back of a knife or your little finger. Sift raising agents with the flour and make sure they are well mixed before adding to other ingredients. The easiest way to do this is to give it a quick whiz with a whisk – electric or a basic balloon whisk.

If you want to turn plain flour into self-raising, add 1 level tsp baking powder for every 125g plain flour. Make sure raising agents are fresh – within their best-before date – or they may fail to produce the desired effect.

Sugar and other sweeteners

Sugar, with its alluring sweetness, enriches the flavour and texture of cakes. Until the mid-1970s, most sugar used for home-baking was refined white, with a small amount of demerara or other brown sugar. But today, there is a glorious array of sugars to choose from. Billington's (see directory, p.244) produce some fabulous unrefined sugars, from light, buttery, fine-grained golden caster sugar to rich, toffee-flavoured dark muscovado. I love these unrefined sugars and I know their warm aromas add depth of flavour and sincerity to my baking.

It is, however, caster sugar that picks up the accolade of most used sugar in home-baking. Its free-flowing small grains are perfect for creaming with butter to make the lightest of sponges. The larger crystals of everyday granulated sugar would take ages to beat to the light and fluffy state required in the creamed cake method. Caster sugar is available in refined (white) or unrefined (golden) varieties, the latter having a mellow, faintly caramelly flavour.

With soft brown and muscovado sugars, you will find they sometimes harden and clump together on storing. If this happens, put the sugar in a basin, cover with a damp tea-towel and leave overnight. Hey presto, in the morning you'll find your sugar will be lump-free and easy-going.

The soft browns With their soft, fine grains, these sugars range in colour from light caramel – ideal for light fruit cakes and chocolate cakes – to rich dark brown, which is perfect for sticky gingerbreads.

The muscovados With approximately 6% molasses, muscovado sugars are richer in natural minerals than the soft browns. Intense and nutty in flavour, light brown muscovado is ideal for light or medium fruit cakes, whereas its dark, toffee-flavoured brother adds colour and depth to rich festive-type fruit cakes.

Demerara Caramel-flavoured golden crystals are this sugar's defining characteristic. It is delicious in tray bakes and biscuits and those recipes where butter and sugar are melted together. Less expensive than the soft browns, demerara is a simple way to introduce the robust distinctive flavour of unrefined sugar.

Molasses and treacle These dark, sweet syrups are by-products of the sugar-making process and to all intents and purposes are the same thing. Extracted from the raw cane during refining, they contain all its nutrients and a great deal of concentrated flavour. Their trademark stickiness is crucial to gingerbreads, but their oily brown-black colour and intense taste bring richness and goodness to other cakes too.

Golden syrup With its unique much-loved flavour, golden syrup is often used in crunchy biscuits and gingerbreads. A little in fruit cakes lends a homely flavour, and helps to keep the cake fresher for longer. Bear in mind that golden syrup is about 40% sweeter than standard sugar, so a spoonful or two is probably all you will need to bring that deep, toffee-ish taste.

Honey This can be used in place of some of the sugar in baking recipes and its moisture-absorbing qualities will help cakes stay fresh for longer. If using, substitute roughly 25% honey for sugar. Reduce the oven temperature slightly to prevent over-browning, as honey burns more easily than sugar.

Flavoured sugars These add subtle fragrance and flavour to your baking. Use them to enrich classic sponge cakes and biscuits – by adding to the mixture, or sprinkling them on after baking. While they can be ridiculously expensive to buy, flavoured sugars are simple to make at home (see overleaf). Caster sugar is the best carrier for delicate aromas such as lavender or rose-scented geranium, whereas soft brown sugar is ideal for more robust flavours such as cinnamon. Unquestionably, the most widely used is vanilla sugar. A close second (well for me at least) is orange sugar, which I like to use in fruit cakes and gingery things. Keep jars of flavoured sugar on the go by perpetually topping them up with more sugar and flavouring.

To make a flavoured sugar, simply place the measured sugar and flavouring in a sealed container and combine thoroughly. A large jam jar will do for lavender and cinnamon sugars (the types you might use only in fairly small amounts), whereas it makes sense to use a much larger container for vanilla and orange sugars or any others that you like to use in quantity.

FLAVOUR	SUGAR	ACTION
Vanilla	Caster, preferably unrefined	Add 2 split vanilla pods to 1kg caster sugar. Leave for at least 2 weeks before use. For a more intense flavour, cut the vanilla pods into small pieces and place in a food processor with a quarter of the sugar. Blend until the pods are ground to a coarse powder. Mix with the remaining sugar.
Orange or lemon	Caster, preferably unrefined	Finely pare some citrus zest and cut into 1mm shreds. Place in a very cool oven or a warm airing cupboard until completely dry. Combine with the sugar, using the peel of 1 entire orange or lemon for every 1kg sugar. Leave for at least 2 weeks before using.
Cinnamon	Light soft brown	Add 1 tsp ground cinnamon for each 100g sugar. You can use this straight away.
Lavender	Caster	Add 1 tsp dried lavender flowers, or half a dozen fresh lavender heads, for every 100g sugar. Leave for a month before using. You can sift it to remove the flower heads before using, if you like.
Rose-scented geranium	Caster	Dry a good handful of rose-scented geranium leaves in a warm place for a couple of days. Layer them in a jar with 1kg sugar. Leave for a couple of weeks before using. This is a lovely sugar to use in simple sponges or in other recipes instead of rose water.

Icing sugar The finest-textured of the sugars, icing sugar is of course perfect for icings – whether water, butter or cream cheese based. In addition, a snowy dusting will finish many cakes, as well as covering up any cracks on the surface. Use white refined if you want a pure white finish. Or, for a delicious, light brown, natural caramel icing, use unrefined icing sugar. A few biscuit recipes call for icing sugar in the mix itself as it gives very light, crisp results (see Jammy dodgers, p.84).

Eggs

This key ingredient contributes moisture, volume, lightness, flavour, colour and nutrition. What's more, eggs come in their own recyclable packaging. Rich in protein, fat and essential vitamins, they really are little wonders. Brown, white, blue or speckled, it really doesn't matter what the shells look like. The most important thing is that the eggs are fresh and have come from healthy free-range hens that have fed and foraged on natural and/or organic food. For cake-making, to get the best out of eggs, they should be used at room temperature. If the weather is particularly cold, warm the eggs by placing them in a bowl of hot but not boiling water for a minute. If these fundamental principles are in place, the rich flavour and deep golden colour of the yolks will be reflected in the finished cake.

All eggs are pretty much the same shape, but their sizes can vary considerably. Commercial egg producers use the following grading:

Very large	73g plus
Large	63–73g
Medium	53–63g
Small	53g and under

And then of course, there are duck and goose eggs, much bigger than hen's, prized for their deep, golden yolks and renowned for the cakes they make.

So how do you know which egg to use? I generally use good medium-sized or smallish large hen's eggs when baking i.e. ones that weigh around 63g.

If you have a supply of small bantam eggs or big goose eggs instead, weigh them with their shells on. Then, bearing in mind the 63g factor, you can work out how many you will need. A medium-sized goose egg is usually equivalent to three 63g hen's eggs, while one monstrous, emerald-green emu egg will replace ten hen's eggs. Admittedly, I've not yet had the opportunity of making a cake with one of these, though three emus live a stone's throw from my house.

P.S. Egg whites freeze well. Place in a small container and label with the number of whites. Or freeze single egg whites in ice-cube trays, then put into a bag, seal and store for up to 6 months. Once thawed they are perfect for making meringues.

Fats
Fat brings flavour and texture to a cake and home-bakers have a choice far removed from the bland, omnipresent palm oils that saturate commercial baked products.

Butter Most often of all, I reach for butter, because the flavour is just incomparable. Unsalted butter, sometimes called sweet butter, is best for baking. Its pure, nutty flavour and soft texture are perfect for baking. However, you can use salted butter if

you prefer – but make sure it's only lightly salted, or the flavour of the finished cake may be adversely affected. (In fact, these days, most butter is only lightly salted.)

For most baking purposes, especially if it needs to be creamed, butter should be soft (though not oily) and at room temperature. Provided it is, you'll find creaming a satisfying task, rather than an exhausting one.

Other fats and butter substitutes You may, for health or dietary reasons, opt to use one of the processed margarine-type fats instead of butter. Indeed, many cake-makers prefer to use these soft, whipped-up emulsions that can be beaten quickly and easily, straight from the fridge, to make quick-mix and unquestionably light sponge cakes. If you do go for margarine, then use one that is non-hydrogenated and therefore free from trans-fatty acids. Look for margarines that state they only use palm oil from a sustainable source.

I rarely use soft margarines myself but I do like to use rapeseed or sunflower oil in some of my baking. These pure vegetable oils are quick and easy to incorporate in muffins, tea breads, some fruit cakes and other recipes that contain a relatively small amount of fat and do not rely on creaming butter to incorporate 'lift' into the mixture. In the spirit of experimentation, I made a Victoria sandwich with sunflower oil, and although it rose and looked the part, the texture was quite dense and the flavour rather unpleasant.

Although little used these days, dripping, the rich sweet fat left after roasting a joint of beef, can be used to replace butter in farmhouse fruit cakes.

Optional extras

With the above basic ingredients in place, do take the time, before you get baking, to consider how other ingredients are brought into play and how they can influence the simplest of cakes.

Citrus fruits The peel or zest of citrus fruit is bursting with fragrant oil that helps to protect and preserve the fruity flesh inside – remove this thin outer layer of waxy skin and within a day or two the fruit shrivels and the flesh inside spoils. Citrus zest will bring acidity and a zesty vibrancy to your baking. Finely grated citrus zest is a valuable ingredient and is frequently added to cakes, biscuits and icings – quite literally for its absolutely fabulous zestiness.

To get the maximum flavour out of citrus zest, add it with the butter: its flavour will be fully released when the butter is pounded to a cream. Use a citrus zester or a fine grater to remove the aromatic zest from the fruit, without including the bitter white pith underneath.

The squeezed juice of citrus fruit has a less pungent and pervasive flavour, but it is very useful for soaking dried fruit and flavouring icings and drizzle toppings.

Candied peel The bitter-sweet citrussy tang of this ingredient contributes to the complex mix of flavours in many fruit cakes and gingery recipes. Made by softening and preserving thick slices of citrus peel in sugar, it can be bought ready diced in small bits (though I find these rather hard with little flavour), or in larger pieces, which can then be cut using a sharp knife to the size you require. To prevent candied peel becoming hard and gristly, store it wrapped in polythene in an airtight container. You can also make your own, which is straightforward and very satisfying.

Homemade candied peel

3 medium unwaxed oranges
3 unwaxed lemons
400g granulated sugar

Scrub the oranges and lemon, then, using a sharp knife, cut the peel from the fruit, removing it in quarters.

Put the citrus peels into a large pan and cover with 2 litres cold water. Bring to the boil and simmer for 5 minutes. Drain, return to the pan and add 1 litre fresh cold water. Bring to the boil and simmer, covered, for a good hour until the peels have softened. Add the sugar and stir until dissolved. Simmer, covered for about 20 minutes. Remove from the heat and leave to stand for 24 hours.

Bring the pan to the boil again. Simmer, uncovered, for about 30 minutes or until the peels have become translucent and most of the liquid has evaporated. Remove from the heat and allow to cool. Using a pair of tongs, remove the peels and place on a wire rack, filling the centres with any remaining syrup.

Pack, when cool, in a sterilised jam jar or airtight container. Cut and use as required. This candied peel will keep unopened for 3–4 months.

P.S. The 'juiced out' shells of citrus fruit can be turned into fragrant fire-lighters. Place on a wire tray in a warm airing cupboard, cool oven or the bottom of an Aga and leave for 2–3 days until the peel has dried out. Keep in a dry place. When laying a fire, pop a few pieces in with the paper and kindling wood. As you light your fire, the volatile, aromatic citrus oils will fill the room with their gorgeous aroma.

Other fresh fruit and vegetables These can add volume, moisture, fibre and nutrients to a cake. Both carrots and apples have long been used in sweet baking, but parsnips, courgettes, rhubarb, pears and other orchard fruits can all be employed to create airily light, mouthwatering cakes. Prepare vegetables and fruit just before adding them to a mixture by grating with a very fine grater or the grating disc on a food processor. Fold into the batter as quickly as possible to prevent discolouration.

Glacé cherries Quite the queen of the preserved fruits in cake-making, these little gems bring a hint of sweet almond flavour along with a succulent yet crunchy texture. Avoid very brightly coloured red cherries for they will almost certainly contain E127 colouring. Natural glacé cherries, although much darker in colour, have a delicate taste.

To prevent cherries sinking to the bottom of a cake, rinse them in a little warm water to remove the sugar syrup (the sugar is the heavy bit). Dry them well, halve and toss in a little flour before using.

Dried fruits With their sweet intense flavours, dried fruits lend character and texture to a cake. They are, of course, simply fresh fruits that have been preserved by drying – either naturally in the sun or in a commercial drying unit.

Conventional dried fruit may contain sulphur dioxide; this is added to keep the colour and halt natural oxidisation. Organic dried fruit is produced without chemical intervention, which usually results in the fruit being much darker and, I think, better flavoured.

When you are buying dried fruit, bear in mind that the plumpest fruits are not necessarily the best. Often the most shrivelled-looking fruits retain the most flavour and, as they are so dehydrated, you get better value for your money. I buy most of my dried fruits from my local health food shop. Crazy Jack (see directory, p.244) produce an excellent organic range, which is available from many health food stores and supermarkets.

When it comes to cake-making, you are most likely to use dried vine fruits and, although technically they are all raisins, they split into three categories:

Currants are small, seedless and intensely sweet. Sometimes called 'raisins of the sun', they are dried black Zante grapes and come mainly from Greece.

Sultanas are pale golden, seedless and succulent. Most of our sultanas come from Turkey.

Raisins are dried white grapes usually of the muscatel variety and are mainly from the USA, Turkey, Greece and Australia.

Aside from this holy trinity, other dried fruits to use in your baking include apricots, dates, figs, prunes, cherries and cranberries.

Coconut The sweet white flesh from the mature fruit of the coconut palm is readily available as grated desiccated coconut and shredded dried coconut, in both sweetened and unsweetened forms. Sweetened desiccated coconut is the product most often used in baking. It brings natural moisture and that unmistakable coconut flavour to a cake. It is imported from many developing countries, but I do like to make sure the coconut I use is from a fair-trade source. Both desiccated and shredded dried coconut can also be lightly toasted and used as a decoration.

Nuts Used whole, chopped or ground, these bring texture, moisture, immense flavour and exceptional nutritional value to a cake. For flavour and freshness, it's best to buy nuts in relatively small quantities. They soon become stale and turn rancid on storing. Buy almonds and hazels with their skins on – they'll have a much better flavour and are less expensive. Once you have cracked the technique of removing their skins (see below), you'll find it a quick and easy job to do.

Chopping nuts is much easier if you warm them slightly first, by tossing them for a minute or so in a frying pan over a medium-low heat, or placing them on a baking tray in a low oven. This simple action will prevent them from shooting all over the place as you chop them. Also, the end result will be much nicer if you chop nuts by hand, rather than use a food processor.

The sweet almond, in the culinary world, is considered the doyenne of nuts. It can be used whole, split, flaked and/or blanched (skin removed), but perhaps its greatest contribution to baking is when it is ground. Ground almonds can be used to replace a proportion of flour and give a cake an appealing moistness without making it too heavy. Bought ready-ground almonds are very fine and delicate, though they need to be used quite quickly as they have a tendency to go stale and rancid. Alternatively, you can grind your own almonds in a food processor; the texture will be a little coarser and the flavour a little fresher (see below). The dark-tan skin of almonds can taste quite bitter and is best removed before using.

To blanch (or skin) almonds: place the nuts in a small bowl, cover with boiling water and leave for 1 minute. Drain, pour on fresh boiling water and leave for another 2–3 minutes. Drain again and set aside until cool enough to handle. Pinch the nuts between your finger and thumb and you will find they will shoot out of their loose, baggy skins at great speed. Dry with a tea-towel or kitchen paper.

Sometimes slivered almonds are called for in a recipe. Indeed using slivered, rather than roughly chopped, nuts will give your baking more style. You can buy slivered almonds or, better still, slice blanched almonds lengthways two or three times into shapely splinters.

Hazelnuts are delicious in cakes, or on top of them, whether whole, chopped or ground. The trees or shrubs are common in the UK and hazelnuts can be foraged from hedgerows and woods. (Note that when cultivated they are called either cobnuts or filberts.) The summer needs to be long and hot to produce good-sized nuts. Not only that, our native squirrels are mindful of nut-collecting time. For this reason, I often find myself relying on imported nuts. Hazels have a thin dark red-brown skin which is best removed before using.

To skin hazelnuts: toast them in a non-stick frying pan over a medium heat, shaking the pan to prevent them from burning, for 3–4 minutes until their skins begin to crack and flake off. Remove from the heat and leave until cool enough to handle. Now this is where the fun starts. Place 8–10 nuts between the palms of your hands. Rub vigorously until the skins flake off and you are left with creamy-yellow naked nuts. Alternatively, you can rub them in a tea-towel.

Walnuts, with their soft, yet crunchy texture, are invaluable either in cakes or used as a decoration on the top. Unlike hazels and almonds, it is unnecessary to skin them. To restore slightly stale walnuts, toss them in a warm small frying pan for a couple of minutes to release their flavoursome oil.

To prepare your own ground nuts: whiz the skinned nuts in a food processor until they are very finely ground. To retain freshness, store the ground nuts in an airtight container and use within 2–3 weeks.

Praline is a sweet nutty confection – lovely sprinkled onto cakes or blended with melted chocolate as a filling or topping. It takes just 10 minutes or so to make. Have ready a lightly oiled baking sheet. Put 125g granulated sugar in a heavy-based saucepan and place over a low heat until the sugar has dissolved to a clear syrup. Add 125g almonds or hazelnuts (skins on). Swirl the pan around until the nuts are evenly coated with the sugar syrup. Continue to cook until the syrup turns nutty brown (watch carefully as it can quickly go too far and start to burn). Tip the mixture onto the oiled baking sheet and leave until cool. Place the cooled praline in a food processor and whiz to a coarse powder. Store in an airtight jar for up to 3 months.

P.S. To remove fragments of shell from a batch of freshly shelled nuts, place the nuts in a large bowl of cold water and the shells will float to the surface.

Spices Rich with the exotic and beguiling essences of their native lands, spices are wonderful additions to many cakes. To get the best flavour from spices, buy them in small quantities and use them up relatively quickly to ensure they are fresh; out-of-date ground spices can be severely lacking in flavour. Many independent health food shops sell spices loose, so you can buy them little and often. Steenbergs (see directory, p.244) have a first-rate range of organic and fair-trade spices and other baking ingredients. Store spices in airtight containers, such as little jam jars.

Cinnamon, with its warming, fragrant tones, is often used in cakes made with orchard fruits. It complements apples particularly well, but also pears and plums.

Nutmeg, with its mellow, sweetly aromatic qualities, is a key ingredient in mixed spice, but it is also lovely to use independently in rich fruit cakes and everyday apple cakes. Nutmeg can be bought ready ground, but I prefer to use it freshly grated from a whole nutmeg kernel.

Mixed spice is a harmonious medley of ground sweet spices. Typically it includes cinnamon, nutmeg, coriander, ginger, allspice and cloves – a perfect mix to add to fruit cakes and spicy biscuits.

Poppy seeds, with their sweet, slightly nutty flavour and distinctive slate-blue colour, give aroma and texture to otherwise plain cakes.

Caraway seeds have been used for centuries in spice cakes, biscuits and breads for their pungent aniseed-like flavour.

Vanilla is used very often in cake-making – its unique mellow, fragrant sweetness being highly prized in no end of recipes. It is available as whole pods, a ground powder or a liquid extract. None of the options are cheap, but investment in pure vanilla is a must in my book. If using extract, make sure it is pure vanilla extract, not a synthetic vanilla 'essence'.

Ginger adds fiery warmth and true spiciness to cakes and biscuits. Ground ginger is commonly used; this is root ginger, dried and ground to a powder. Sticky glacé stem ginger and preserved stem ginger in syrup can also be chopped and added to cakes to give bite, texture and flavour.

Salt Although not strictly necessary, a little salt will fine-tune and enhance the final flavour. It may appear somewhat contradictory to use unsalted butter and then add salt, but I can assure you, the pinch of salt usually specified in recipes is far less than the amount contained in salted butter. Use a fine-grained sea salt.

Chocolate Lending a divine smooth richness and untold seductiveness, chocolate is quintessential in baking. Don't we all love a chocolate cake? In cake-making, it is used in both powder form (cocoa) and as a solid (chocolate). Cocoa powder is rich in flavour and colour, but rather bitter; it is ground from the dried solids of the fermented cocoa bean after the cocoa butter has been removed.

Chocolate itself contains cocoa solids and cocoa butter, and often sugar as well. It is the proportion of cocoa solids that determines the grade of chocolate. Plain (dark) chocolate ranges between 35% cocoa solids (the legal minimum) and 100% (for a very dark, bitter bar). White chocolate doesn't contain any cocoa solids but is a blend of cocoa butter, milk and sugar, resulting in a very low melting point.

I like to use a good plain, semi-sweet or bitter-sweet chocolate with a cocoa solid content around 60–70%, which yields a delicious smoothness with a relatively low melting point. Green & Black's (see directory, p.244) produce excellent well-priced organic cocoa powder and chocolate. If you are using really intense 100% dark chocolate, such as Willie's (www.williescacao.com), use roughly 30% less than the recipe states.

Flowers and herbs Look no further than the summer garden or hedgerow to find flowers and herbs to add heady or aromatic fragrance to your baking. The early-summer hedgerows, more often than not, are alive with the creamy white blossom of elderflowers. A little later, the summer garden will provide breathtaking scents from roses, lavender and jasmine, while the leaves from aromatic herbs such as rose-scented geraniums, lemon verbena and peppermint can be used to impart their unique sweet, fresh savour to your baking.

Simply steep the flowers or foliage in a little water to add to simple sponges and icings, or lightly sweeten to make a fragrant sugar syrup to drizzle over freshly baked cakes (see Scent from heaven cake, p.160).

Likewise, more concentrated, yet still delicately perfumed, orange flower and rose waters add blissful tones to fruit or almondy cakes and marzipan. These can be bought from specialist baking suppliers such as Steenbergs (see directory, p.244).

Baking methods

There are five basic ways to combine ingredients for a cake. These methods all have similar aims: to thoroughly blend dry, lighter ingredients with moist, heavier ones and to incorporate air into the batter in order to give lift and lightness.

Rubbing-in method

This is often used for biscuit-making and for cakes that contain little fat. Butter or other fat is cut into small pieces, then added to sifted flour and lightly rubbed in with the fingertips until the mixture resembles breadcrumbs. You will get much better results if your hands are cool, and if you work the mixture lightly, lifting the crumbs high to keep the blend soft, airy and free-flowing.

Creaming method

This is probably the most widely used cake-making technique and it is best employed for large egg- and butter-rich cakes, such as Victoria sandwiches and some fruit cakes. Softened butter or margarine is first thoroughly beaten, or 'creamed', until light and fluffy, then fine-grained caster sugar is added. The key to success (so please don't skimp) is then to cream the butter and sugar together energetically to create a mass of tiny air bubbles. Once surrounded with an egg-based batter and baked, these bubbles 'set' and provide the light, airy structure of the cake. It is important to make sure all the gritty bits of sugar are completely blended into the creamy mix, so always scrape down the sides of the bowl a couple of times while creaming.

Creaming properly by hand will take 10–15 minutes. If you are using a hand-held electric whisk, you should allow 5–6 minutes; with a free-standing electric mixer, it will take about 4 minutes. If using an electric whisk, start off on the lowest speed, increasing to moderate once the butter and sugar are thoroughly combined.

Whisking method

This technique involves vigorously beating eggs and sugar to incorporate air until a thick, creamy mousse is formed, then folding in sifted flour, and sometimes a little melted butter. It is particularly used for light sponges and fatless cakes, such as Swiss rolls. The egg-and-sugar mousse is very delicate and care must be taken to minimise the loss of volume when folding in the flour. Before you begin, do make sure that your bowl and whisk are spotlessly clean, as any grease in the bowl will prevent the eggs from whisking up properly.

If you are using a balloon whisk or an old-fashioned hand whisk, the eggs and sugar need to be placed in a heatproof bowl sat over a pan of just-off-the-boil water (don't allow the bowl to touch the water). The heat from the steam helps the sugar to dissolve and thickens the egg very slightly. If, however, you are using a hand-held

electric whisk or free-standing electric mixer, it is not necessary to do this. Having said that, you will certainly find that placing the bowl over hot water when using a hand-held electric whisk speeds up the operation.

Melting or warming method

This is frequently used when making damp cakes, such as gingerbreads and tray bakes, as well as crunchy biscuits. It is a lovely, straightforward technique that involves melting butter, syrups, sugar and liquids together before adding them, often with a beaten egg or two, to the dry ingredients.

Blitz or 'all-in-one' method

The simplest and fastest way of making a cake, whereby all the ingredients are beaten together with an electric mixer for no more than 1½–2 minutes. This method is ideal if you want to whip up a sponge cake very quickly, but success relies on all the ingredients being at room temperature when you begin. (This is one instance when soft margarine wins hands down over butter, because it can be used straight from the fridge.) Though quick and easy to make, I always feel that a blitzed cake lacks the dignified demeanour of a traditionally creamed one.

Lining tins

Greasing and/or lining baking tins will help any reluctant or shy cakes to be released after baking. I find butter the best greasing medium. I prefer it to processed margarines, while I've found oils do not always give a completely non-stick surface. You can use either a bit of butter wrapper with a knob of soft butter on it, or dab a pastry brush in a little melted butter and paint over the base and sides of the tin.

For most cakes, I simply grease the sides of the tin with softened butter, then smear a little on the base to just hold a piece of baking parchment in place. Gluten-free cakes are more likely to stick, so make sure you grease the tins for these very well. Richer, deeper fruit cakes demand a bit more comfort so run a piece of baking parchment around the sides of the tin too. For cakes with crumbly toppings such as Somerset cider cake (p.168) or Hugh's fresh cherry cake (p.174), do make sure you use a springform tin or one with a loose bottom so you can remove it easily.

Dusting the tin with flour after greasing it gives fatless sponges a crisper and more defined outline and will also help them to cling and 'climb' up the side of the tin in the oven. Use flour on its own, or mixed with an equal quantity of caster sugar. Dust the flour round the inside of the greased tin until it is evenly coated, removing any excess by shaking the tin upside down over the sink. For chocolate cakes, dust the tin with a mix of cocoa powder and sugar.

Lining a round tin

For the base, either use a pre-cut baking parchment circle (available from independent hardware stores and supermarkets) or make your own by placing the tin on a sheet of baking parchment, drawing around the base and cutting out with scissors.

For the sides, cut a strip of baking parchment approximately 2.5cm longer than the circumference of the tin and about 3cm wider than the height of the tin. Fold down a 1.5cm strip along one long edge, then unfold and use scissors to snip to the fold line, roughly at 2.5cm intervals. Press the strip around the inside of the greased tin, allowing the frilled edge to fit snugly around the base. Place the baking parchment base disc on top. Look out for narrow rolls of baking parchment (10cm wide), which are just the job for lining sides; these are available from Lakeland (see directory, p.244).

P.S. For garland or ring moulds, there is no need to line. Simply grease the tin well with butter. Turn the cake out 5–10 minutes after removing from the oven.

Lining a square tin or Swiss roll tin

Measure the base of the tin, adding on the depth of the sides plus an extra 1cm. Cut a piece of baking parchment this size. Place the tin in the middle of the paper and mark each of the corners. Then cut from the outer-edge corners of the baking parchment to the marked corners in the centre. Dab a little butter on the base and the sides of the tin (this is just to hold the paper in place). Ease the paper into the tin, folding the diagonally cut flappy ends neatly around each corner. For deep-sided tins you may need to smear a tiny bit of butter to keep these pieces in place.

To line a loaf tin

Use the method above or, more simply, just cut a piece of baking parchment long enough to cover the base and the long sides, then liberally grease the unlined ends. If the cake is reluctant to release, then run a small knife around the edge of the unlined ends.

P.S. To give a hint of perfume to light summer sponges, place 3–4 sweet scented geranium or lemon verbena leaves on the lined base of the tin. Remove them from the baked cake when it is turned out.

Baking expressions

As time goes by, and with increasing experience, you'll begin to have baking conversations with yourself: *'Needs a little longer'* or *'Mmmm, that looks good'.* These unconscious thoughts will appear to be fitting for whatever stage the cake is at. However, there are a few customary terms which repeatedly crop up in baking methods and it's well worth understanding their meanings:

Curdling

Curdling describes when a beaten mixture breaks down into tiny grainy curds. It can occur when eggs are added to creamed butter and sugar, for one of three reasons. Firstly, it could be that the butter and sugar have not been creamed thoroughly and the sugar is still gritty when the egg is added (see the creaming method, p.37). Secondly, it may be that the eggs are too cold. If you are using eggs straight from the fridge, warm them up by placing them in a bowl of hot but not boiling water for a minute. Finally, curdling can occur when the eggs are added too quickly to the creamed butter and sugar.

It is to prevent curdling that you are often told to add 1 tbsp flour with each egg, and to ensure an egg is thoroughly beaten in before adding the next. Another trick to help avoid curdling is to add 1 tbsp flour before the first egg. A curdled mixture cannot hold air well and will result in a heavy cake. If, despite all precautions, your mixture does curdle, add 1 tbsp sifted flour to prevent it breaking down any more.

Folding in

This is a gentle cutting and folding action used to incorporate light ingredients into a heavier mixture. This term most frequently applies when adding flour to creamed or whisked mixtures. It is also the technique used to incorporate whisked egg whites into a cake mixture. Folding should be done using either a large metal spoon or a rubber spatula.

To fold in, you need to cut vertically through the mix with a deft, clean stroke, while at the same time rotating the bowl a quarter-turn with your other hand, bringing the spoon out and 'folding' the mixture over on itself. This gentle repeated action will turn the ingredients over on top of each other, combining them without losing too much of that precious trapped air.

Dropping consistency

This describes the texture of a cake mixture when a spoonful of it will fall from the spoon when it is tapped on the side of the bowl or lightly shaken. A soft dropping consistency is the stage at which a mixture will drop from the spoon by itself when the spoon is tipped.

Ribbon consistency

This is the term used to define when a whisked mixture is very thick, light in colour and falls away in a ribbon-like fashion when the beaters are lifted up out of the mix. It is most often applied to whisking eggs and sugar together, for example when making a Genoese or whisked sponge.

Turning out

This simply means removing a freshly baked cake from its tin. Turning out onto a footed wire rack allows heat to escape quickly and makes for a lighter cake. Light sponge cakes need to be left in their tins for 5–10 minutes after coming out of the oven, to settle and firm up, whereas more robust fruit and drizzle cakes are often left in their tins until cold.

To turn out a cake, place a wire rack over the top of the tin and invert both the cake and the rack then, with care, lift the tin off. (To prevent a criss-cross grid marking the top of the cake, place a clean folded tea-towel on the rack first.) Remove any lining paper and then turn the cake back the right way up with the help of a second rack. With experience, you will find you'll be able to use your hand for this stage, so you won't require a second rack.

Cake-makers' tips

This handful of baking tips should help your cake-making session to run smoothly. Enjoy your baking – your pleasure will be reflected in the finished cake.

Get organised before you start to bake Weigh out all the ingredients for the recipe and put them on a tray. For recipes with lots of ingredients, tick them off as you go. There are two advantages to doing this. The first is that you won't leave anything out (I speak from experience: my Christmas cake has, on more than one occasion, been missing the odd ingredient). The second plus is that your cupboard door handles won't get sticky.

Before you begin, sift the flour with any salt, raising agent or spices This will aerate and separate the fine flour particles and evenly distribute the other dry ingredients.

Place a damp, folded tea-towel underneath the bowl This will prevent it from slipping or skidding on the worktop.

Get to know your oven Resolve any idiosyncrasies it might have. Is it hot or cool or decidedly moody on a Monday morning? Adjust baking times and temperatures accordingly. More often than not, the most favourable cake-baking temperature is 180°C/Gas mark 4 and this is well worth remembering.

Once the cake is in the oven *Do not* open the door until at least three-quarters of the way through the recommended baking time. Open it too soon and both you and the cake will get a sinking feeling as that magical rise disappears, never to return. Remember too, if baking your cake in a larger than recommended tin, the cooking time will be less. Conversely, in a smaller tin, the cake will be deeper and take longer. Indeed, you may well need to reduce the heat a little towards the end of baking, or cover the top with a double thickness of baking parchment to prevent it browning too much while the centre finishes cooking.

Avoid any aerobic exercise near the oven This includes children playing hop-scotch on the kitchen tiles. Cakes thrive in a secure atmosphere. Bumps and thumps, in a baking environment, will frighten the cake and there is a good chance it will sink.

Cakes, when done, will shrink away slightly from the tin or the lining paper For creamed and whisked mixtures, the cake should spring back into shape when lightly pressed with your fingertip. For fruit cakes and heavier cakes, a fine skewer or small, sharp knife inserted into the centre of the cake should come out clean.

Recipe essentials

For the recipes in this book, unless otherwise stated:
- Spoon measurements are level.
- Eggs, with shell on, weigh approximately 63g.
- Bake your cake in the centre of the oven.
- Cooking times are a guide, not written in stone. Check your cake three-quarters of the way through the suggested cooking time.
- For fan-assisted ovens, reduce the given temperature by 10–20°C depending on your oven.

Storage

Homemade cakes have best-before dates, just like shop-bought ones. I have recommended a conservative keeping time for each recipe in this book. In general though, cakes tend to fall into four types:

Muffins and fatless sponges These are best eaten freshly baked; I don't mean scoffing the lot as soon as they are out of the oven, but certainly eat within a couple of days.

Vegetable/fresh fruit-baked cakes The high moisture content of these cakes means they should be stored in a cool place and eaten within 3–4 days.

Creamed cakes (For example, a Victoria sponge.) Best eaten within 5–6 days.

Dried fruit-based cakes These are the long-term keepers and, more often than not, actually improve with time. Wrap these cakes lightly in greaseproof paper and store in an airtight container or cake tin.

Most cakes freeze well and slicing and freezing them is one way to avoid uncontrolled cake consumption and have ready a wedge or two for a lunch box.

Cakes are best kept in airtight containers or cake storage tins. When used over a period of years cake tins will become much loved and well respected 'friends' in your kitchen. Sometimes it can be a bit of a tight squeeze to transfer a finished (especially a decorated cake) into a tin. A nifty and easy way to do this is to cut a strip of greaseproof paper about 15cm x 50cm. Place the cake in the centre of the strip and use the ends to carefully lift and then lower the cake into the tin. Leave the paper strip in place, either folding the ends over the cake or the outside edge of the tin. You can then use the ends to lift the cake out of the tin when required.

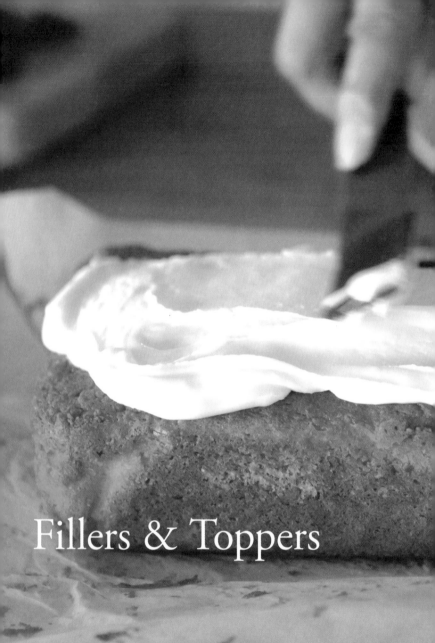

Fillers & Toppers

I'm not an expert cake decorator, but I do love to prettify some of my cakes. Unquestionably, there are some cakes which can be transformed into little seductresses with a touch or two of glitz or glamour. However, I generally steer clear of too much tarting up. I much prefer to keep my cakes naturally beautiful with just a few simple decorative touches – some arty feather icing, perhaps, or a few well-chosen dainty flowers to enhance their inherent charm.

Simple icings are the obvious choice. A coating of soft, sweet buttercream, gently smoothed across the top of a cake, is often enough, but a drizzle, which is poured over a cake, is even easier and its essence permeates right through to the core.

Nature offers up a number of amazing decorative gifts too. Fresh, fragrant edible flowers, such as primroses, marigolds, borage and roses, will beautify a simple iced sponge cake, while the juice of fresh summer berries – used in place of water in icings – gives outstanding flavour and colour. Likewise, the heavenly scents of aromatic flowers and herbs can be captured by infusing them in liquids, their vivacity bringing unexpected pleasure to the simplest of toppings. And the intricate patterns and beautiful shapes of leaves can be transferred to chocolate to make feather-light edible foliage.

Keeping decorations simple makes your life easier and means the cake itself remains the focus of attention.

Fillers

There is a fine line between what constitutes a cake filler and a topper. Many of these delectable fillers will feel equally at home on top of the cake as they do sandwiched in between the layers. Conversely, you will find some of the soft toppers will adapt very comfortably to the role of a filler. The moral of this is that it gives you the chance to do a little mix and matching, as well as using the ingredients you happen to have to hand.

Vanilla buttercream

This classic all-rounder doubles as a velvety smooth topper and filler in many cakes. It can work solo or partner up on the adhering job with a few spoonfuls of hold-fast jam. The rich, sweet taste of buttercream works particularly well with plain cakes and is perfect for topping cup or fairy cakes.

To fill a 20cm sandwich cake or top 12 fairy cakes
60g unsalted butter, softened and cut into small pieces
125g icing sugar, sifted
½ tsp vanilla extract

Place the butter in a mixing bowl and, either using a wooden spoon or a hand-held electric whisk, beat until creamy. Incorporate the icing sugar in three lots, beating well before adding the next. When it is all added the mixture should be a light cream. Finally mix in the vanilla extract.

Variations

Chocolate Replace 25g of the icing sugar with cocoa powder.

Coffee Add 1 tbsp coffee essence or 1 tbsp instant coffee dissolved in 1 tbsp hot water and cooled.

Nut Add 75g finely chopped nuts or 2–3 tbsp praline (see p.33).

Honey Replace half the icing sugar with 2 tbsp runny honey.

Jammy fillers

Whole-fruit jam or fruity jammy jellies are a blissful and easy way to glue a sandwich cake together, as well as a resourceful use of homemade preserves. Although red jams are customarily used, there is no prescriptive flavour to use, so choose your favourite. Gooseberry, for example, works particularly well in a cake topped with elderflower-infused glacé icing.

Lemon curd

Freshly made lemon curd makes a delectable filling for sponge cakes and Swiss rolls. You can make it while the cake is baking – it really doesn't take long. Add a crushed meringue (see p.112) to the finished curd for a crunchy lemon-meringue filling.

To fill a 20cm cake or Swiss roll (with some to spare)
Finely grated zest and juice of 1 large unwaxed lemon
75g caster sugar
50g unsalted butter
2 eggs, well beaten

Have ready a pan of barely simmering water. Put all the ingredients, except the eggs, into a heatproof bowl that will sit snugly on the pan without touching the water. Place the bowl over the water and, stirring once or twice, leave until the butter has just melted. Briskly whisk in the eggs using a balloon whisk, until thoroughly combined into the buttery lemon mixture. Scrape the sides down and whisk occasionally until the mixture is glossy and thickened. Either cool in the bowl and use immediately to fill a cooled cake, or pour into a couple of small clean jam jars, seal with a metal lid and store in the fridge; use within 2 weeks.

Meringutan

This is my quirky name for a delightful fillin?
Simply blend a crushed meringue (see p.11
cream to give you enough to layer two 20c
three-layer cake.

Caramel cream

A glorious confection to squeeze betweer
simply (and I hope you don't think this a
Place a tin of condensed milk on a folde(
in a deep stainless-steel saucepan. Cover completely w....
to simmering point and keep it at a low simmer for 1½–2 hours – the long-
cooked, the thicker and darker the caramel will be. Make sure you keep the pan
topped up with hot water. Remove from the heat and leave the tin in the saucepan
until it is completely cold before opening.

It's worth preparing several tins at a time – to save on fuel. Once cooked, the
unopened tins will keep for up to a year, but do remember to mark the cans so you
know what they are.

Toppers

The topping, or th?
rather special an?
in many cases
cake. Do
cake wil
are th
D

finishing touch on a cake, will turn any cake into something eye-catching. Just a simple dusting of icing sugar will do the trick while a specially prepared icing will flatter and bring harmony to the ake sure the cake is completely cool before filling or topping it – a warm soften the mix and it will drip and ooze all over the place. The exceptions ose cakes that are baked with their toppings already in place, for instance the ndee cake and those with crumbly streusel-type toppings.

In addition to the velvety smooth icings used to coat the tops and sides of cakes, the true finishing touches are special adornments you choose to decorate the cake. These could be a boxful of coloured cake candles, lit to celebrate a birthday or anniversary. If you take a glance around the garden or hedgerow from springtime through to autumn, you will find edible flowers and other natural and earthy decorations to gather for free. Then again, a handful of whole or chopped nuts will give a lovely finish to many cakes.

Nonetheless, a few well-chosen shop-bought sugar cake decorations certainly won't go amiss, and will allow you to speedily pretty up freshly baked cakes and biscuits. I like the fair-trade chocolate drops and the vermicelli decorations from Steenbergs (see directory, p.244) and sugary flowers (particularly the violets) from Cakes, Cookies and Crafts (see directory, p.244).

Caster sugar

A simple sprinkling of caster sugar will give freshly baked biscuits and many cakes their finishing touch. In fact this free-flowing sugar is the classic topping for the ever-favourite Victoria sandwich.

Icing sugar

Dusted lightly over the top of a cake, this superfine sugar powder is often sufficient to give an attractive finish. Alternatively, paper doilies or homemade stencils can be used to create a simple or intricate pattern – just place the doily or stencil on top of the cake and dust with icing sugar. Remove the paper very carefully to reveal an instant work of art.

An equal mix of sifted cocoa powder and icing sugar can be used to give a lovely chocolatey finish.

Glacé icing

This straightforward icing, also known as 'water icing', sets to form a crisp surface, but doesn't become hard. The trick is in getting this ever-so-simple icing 'just right'. Too thick, and the icing will not be glistening and glossy; too thin and it will run all over the place. Add less liquid than you think you need; you can always add more. Keep it pure and white, or dress it up with fresh fruit juice, coffee, chocolate, coconut – whatever takes your – or your cake's – fancy.

To top a 20cm round or 18cm square cake or 12 cup cakes
250g icing sugar
About 2 tbsp hot water or flavouring (see variations)

Sift the icing sugar into a mixing bowl. Add 1 tbsp of the liquid to start with and then a little at a time, beating until the mixture is smooth and glossy and thick enough to coat the back of the spoon. Adjust, if necessary, with a drop more water or a little more sifted icing sugar.

Variations

Citrus Use 2 tbsp freshly squeezed lemon, orange or lime juice.

Smooth berry Macerate 75g crushed ripe raspberries or strawberries with 1 tsp icing sugar. Leave until the juices begin to run, and then pass through a sieve to remove the pips.

Whole berry Simply crush or blend 75g berries of your choice to a purée, or use 2 tbsp fruit coulis.

Elderflower Replace 1 tbsp of the water with 1 tbsp elderflower cordial.

Rosehip Replace 1 tbsp of the water with 1 tbsp rosehip cordial.

Coffee Dissolve 1 tbsp instant coffee in 2 tbsp hot water, or use 2 tbsp very strong filter coffee.

Earl Grey or jasmine tea Infuse 1 tea bag in 50ml boiling water, using sufficient to mix to the required texture.

Caramel Simply use unrefined icing sugar.

Chocolate Replace 1 tbsp of the icing sugar with 2 tbsp drinking chocolate or 1 tbsp sifted cocoa powder.

Coconut Replace 1–2 tbsp of the icing sugar with desiccated coconut; this will give you a textured icing.

Feather icing

This is my party piece! It's incredibly simple, but very effective. You will need two different colours of glacé icing – one to coat the cake and another one to feather with. I generally keep the main icing white, then use a strong or vivid colour for the feathering bit. You can use natural food colouring, of course, but a drop or two of blackcurrant cordial or fresh raspberry juice works just as well. Now this is where enterprise comes into play by using, if you like, some fairly whacky colours to feather up your cake.

To cover a 20cm round cake
250g quantity of white Glacé icing (see p.55)
A little natural food colouring

First, take a good tablespoonful of the icing and colour with the food colouring. Place this in a small plastic bag, pushing it into one corner, and set aside. Then, smoothly coat the top of the cake with the white glacé icing. Next, snip off the very tip of the icing-filled point of the plastic bag. Pipe the feathering icing in thin lines across the cake. Now, using the tip of a knife or a skewer, score parallel lines across the piped lines from one side of the cake to the other, alternating directions to create a soft feather-like pattern.

Citrus frosting

A lively topping for plain sponges or cup cakes. The crunchy sugar stays on top while the citrus syrup soaks in. Try using a citrus liqueur in place of half or all the juice.

To top a 20cm round, 18cm square or 12cm x 25cm loaf cake
Juice of 1 lemon, small orange, lime or tangerine (about 50ml)
125g granulated sugar

Mix the citrus juice with the sugar and set aside for 10 minutes. Spoon over the slightly cooled cake before the sugar has fully dissolved.

Cream cheese topping

This is an all-time great for carrot cakes, banana cakes and muffins. Do use a full-fat cream cheese: low-fat ones result in a sloppy icing that runs off the cake.

To top a 20cm round cake or 10 large muffins
100g full-fat cream cheese
25g unsalted butter, softened and cut into small pieces
150–175g icing sugar, sifted
1 tsp vanilla extract or orange flower water, or
the finely grated zest of 1 unwaxed orange or lemon

Beat the cream cheese and butter together until smooth. Add the icing sugar and any flavouring and beat until the mixture is very light and creamy. Cover and refrigerate for an hour or so to firm up before using.

Yoghurt and white chocolate topping

A soft, smooth covering for many cakes, including sponges, carrot cake, ginger cake and cup cakes.

To top a 20cm cake or 18–20 cup cakes
100g white chocolate, broken into small pieces
50–100ml full-fat plain yoghurt

Put the chocolate into a small heatproof bowl. Place over a pan of barely simmering water, without allowing the bowl to touch the water, and leave until the chocolate has just melted. Remove from the heat and beat in sufficient yoghurt to give a smooth, creamy topping. Rest in the fridge for 30 minutes before using.

Marzipan

This timeless nutty confection is somewhat exceptional because it fills and tops, as well as being used for making decorations. Homemade marzipan only takes a few minutes to prepare and it is a thousand times nicer than the bought stuff. It's traditionally made with ground almonds but there is no reason why cashews, hazelnuts or walnuts cannot be used – simply blitz whole skinned nuts (see p.32) in a food processor until they are finely ground.

Marzipan keeps well so you can prepare it in advance and have it to hand when you want to cover a Christmas cake, bake a stollen, sandwich it into a Simnel cake, wrap up a Battenberg or mould it into decorative shapes.

To thickly cover the top and sides of an 18cm round cake
1 medium egg
1 tbsp brandy, whisky or orange liqueur
125g caster sugar
125g icing sugar, sifted
250g ground almonds

Break the egg into a large bowl. Add the alcohol and whisk well together. Add the caster sugar, icing sugar and ground almonds and mix to a stiff paste. Sprinkle your work surface with a little icing sugar, then turn the almond paste out onto it. Knead until the marzipan is soft and smooth (your hands will be soft too). Seal the marzipan in a plastic bag and store in the fridge until required.

To marzipan a round or square cake To cover the top of the cake, take roughly half of the marzipan and place it on a sheet of greaseproof paper lightly dusted with icing sugar. Roll out the marzipan so that it is about 1cm thick and a little larger than the diameter of the cake. Lightly brush the top of the cake with either a little lightly beaten egg white or warmed sieved apricot jam. The easiest way to put the marzipan on the cake is to invert the cake onto the marzipan and give it a good thwack. Trim away the excess marzipan round the edge of the cake before re-inverting and placing on a cake board.

To cover the side of the cake, measure the depth and the circumference of the cake – a piece of string is a handy way to do this. Roll out the remaining marzipan to fit; you may find it easiest to do this in two sections. Brush the sides of the cake with egg white or warm sieved apricot jam and press the marzipan band(s) in place. Use either a straight-sided jam jar or drinking glass to run around the edge of the cake to smooth the sides and fix firmly in place.

Leave the cake in a cool, dry place for 2–3 days to allow the marzipan to dry before applying icing.

To toast marzipan on a rich fruit cake Either just top or completely cover the cake with marzipan (see above). Roll out any leftover marzipan to approximately a 5mm thickness. Use biscuit cutters to cut out shapes: snowflakes, hearts, stars, etc. Brush the cake with lightly beaten egg yolk, then position the marzipan shapes on the top. Brush these with egg yolk too. Place in the oven, preheated to 200°C/Gas mark 6, and bake for about 15 minutes to toast – don't forget it! For a cake only topped with marzipan, tie a band of double-thickness greaseproof paper around the side of the cake to protect it and prevent it from catching.

To colour marzipan Place it on a clean, dry surface dusted with icing sugar. Flatten the marzipan with a rolling pin, and dab a little of the required colouring in the centre. Fold it over a couple of times and roll out again. Repeat the process of folding and rolling until the colour is evenly distributed through the marzipan.

To make marzipan shapes Lightly dust the work surface with icing sugar and roll out the marzipan to approximately a 5mm thickness, then use biscuit cutters to cut out shapes. Alternatively, you can mould shapes, such as vegetables, fruits, flowers, etc., by hand. Just 50g of marzipan will make a bunch of carrots any grocer would be proud to sell. You can use everyday kitchen utensils and store-cupboard ingredients to add texture and finish. For instance, roll moulded oranges over a fine grater or simply use a sharp knife to score lines around the bodies of shapely carrots. Leave on a wire rack for 2–3 days to dry.

Royal icing

As its name suggests, this icing is reserved for top-notch celebration cakes. It's traditionally spread so smoothly that the surface is like a coating of perfect virgin snow, or swirled and lifted to resemble snow peaks. I rarely use royal icing, except to whip up a chaotic snowy scene on my Christmas cake.

To thickly cover the top and sides of a 20cm round or 18cm square cake
2 egg whites
500g icing sugar, sifted
1 tsp lemon juice or orange flower water
1 tsp glycerine (optional, but stops the icing becoming brittle)

Place the egg whites in a large mixing bowl and whisk lightly. Incorporate the icing sugar a spoonful at a time until the mixture falls in a thick ribbon from a spoon. Stir in the flavouring and glycerine if using, then, using either a wooden spoon or a hand-held electric whisk, beat until the icing will stand up in soft peaks. Cover with a damp cloth and leave for roughly 15 minutes to allow any air bubbles to rise to the surface. Cover the top and the sides of the cake with the icing. For an ultra-smooth finish, dip a palette knife into a jug of very hot water to work over the cake, or do as I do and roughly swirl over and rough up with the blade of a knife or a fork.

Fondant icing

Although there are several good proprietary fondant icing sugars on the market (that include in the ingredients a little dried glucose), this really is a lovely icing to add to your repertoire. The lemon in this recipe cuts cleanly through the sweet icing, but by all means ring the changes by replacing both water and lemon juice with other fruity flavours: fresh orange juice, fruity squash or even blitzed summer berries.

To cover a 20cm round cake
2 tbsp glucose syrup (obtainable from chemists)
4 tbsp water
4 tbsp lemon juice
800–850g icing sugar

Have ready a pan of simmering water. Put the glucose syrup, water and lemon juice in a heatproof bowl that will fit snugly over the pan without touching the water. Sift in the icing sugar and beat with a balloon whisk until well combined. Sit the bowl on the pan and heat gently until the mixture is thick and glossy. Remove from the pan and let cool to roughly blood temperature (37°C). When ready to use, place the cake or cakes on a wire rack over a tray or a piece of baking parchment. Pour the icing onto the centre of the cake and allow it to spread over the top and down the sides. Any excess can be scraped from underneath, re-warmed and used again.

Chocolate icing

Smooth, rich and delicious, chocolate icing will dreamily top off any plain, chocolate or coffee cake. Melted chocolate on its own won't do – it sets into a brittle coating that will crack and splinter. A proportion of butter will keep it meltingly soft.

To top a 20cm cake
100g dark chocolate, broken into small pieces
50g unsalted butter, cut into small pieces

Have ready a small pan of simmering water. Place the chocolate in a small heatproof bowl, sit over the pan (make sure it doesn't touch the water) and allow the chocolate to almost completely melt. Just before the last pieces disappear, remove the bowl from the heat. It's important not to get the chocolate too hot, or overwork it; either can cause it to 'split' into grainy solids and a fatty liquid (when it won't be good for anything). Little by little, add the butter, beating until the mixture is smooth and glossy. Set aside for 5–10 minutes to thicken up before spreading over your cake.

Variations

Mocha Add 1 tsp coffee granules when melting the chocolate.

Boozy Fold in 1 tbsp Cointreau, Grand Marnier or brandy once the chocolate and butter are combined and have cooled a little.

Chocolate fudge icing

This soft, mousse-like filling is just the thing to turn a chocolate cake into perfection. Use it also to cover cup cakes or to fill and top a Victoria sandwich or coffee cake.

To fill and top a 20cm cake
150g plain or semi-sweet chocolate, broken into small pieces
75g unsalted butter, diced
2 tbsp milk
3 egg yolks
150g icing sugar, sifted

Put the chocolate, butter and milk into a medium heatproof bowl. Place over a pan of just-simmering water until the chocolate and butter have melted – the mixture should be warm but not hot. Remove from the heat and beat until smooth. Add the egg yolks, one at a time, beating until well combined. Add the sugar, a third at a time, beating to a thick, smooth spreading consistency. Use as required.

Chocolate ganache

Bitter, dark chocolate is normally used for this smooth, creamy classic, but it is also delicious made with a semi-sweet milk or even a creamy white chocolate.

To cover a 20cm cake
125ml double cream
125g dark chocolate, broken into small pieces

Place the cream in a small saucepan and heat very gently until very hot but not boiling. Add the broken chocolate pieces and beat with a wooden spoon until the chocolate has melted and the mixture is smooth. Pour into a clean bowl and set aside to cool. Use at room temperature to pour over a cake, or chill until cold and then whip for a silky chocolate cream to fill, top or smother all over the cake.

Variation
Chocolate crème fraîche (or yoghurt) topping In a similar vein, you can make a lovely chocolate topping by mixing cooled, melted chocolate or chocolate hazelnut spread into the same quantity of plain yoghurt or crème fraîche.

Chocolate leaves

Edible chocolate leaves, moulded from fresh leaves, will cheer up any number of cakes, big or small. Use robust non-toxic leaves with their stems attached – rose, blackberry and bay leaves all work well. Thickly coat the underside of the leaf with melted chocolate, making sure you do not get any on the top side (otherwise it will be difficult to remove). Place on baking parchment and allow to dry completely before peeling off the leaves to reveal perfect chocolate leaves.

Edible flowers

From shrinking violets found in April, nestling in sheltered corners, to late summer's bounty of sensuous garden lavender, many flowers can be snitched away to lavish upon iced or otherwise unadorned cakes. Do take care though, just because a flower is edible, it doesn't mean it tastes good. Camomile, for example, is lovely in tea but bitter on a cake. Stick to familiar faces such as primroses, roses, borage, jasmine, violas, nasturtiums, cornflowers, sage or tiny thyme flowers. I like honeysuckle blooms too – but please remember the berries are poisonous. If you are unsure about whether or not a flower is edible, then do check it out before using. The freshness and verve of these natural decorations will bring free spirit and joy to your cakes. And you can extend their lives by crystallising them in sugar (see overleaf). Store them away and they can bring new life to your baking, even in deep winter.

Crystallised flowers

For some, preparing these may seem a bit of a fiddle, but the time spent gathering and preparing the flowers pales into insignificance when you consider their lasting ethereal beauty. Primroses, violets, violas, apple blossom, rose petals and borage all respond well to the crystallising process. However, in all cases, success depends on both the flowers and the sugar being perfectly dry. Pick the flowers on a dry, sunny day when they are fully open. Remove the stalks.

Pour a lightly beaten (but not frothy) egg white into a saucer. Have another saucer of caster sugar beside it. Using tweezers, dip the flower heads or petals first into the egg white and then into the sugar. Use a fine paintbrush to tease the sugar into any crinkles and hollows within the flower. Shake off any excess sugar before laying the flowers on a sheet of baking parchment. Place in a warm, dry and airy spot to dry for 24–48 hours.

When fully dry, store the crystallised flowers carefully between layers of baking parchment or greaseproof paper in an airtight container.

Angelica

When candied, angelica is rather like a green goddess to the cake-maker. Its slender green stems can be slivered and sliced and used with stunning effect on simple iced cakes or festive glacé-fruit topped cakes. If you have access to young, fresh angelica stems (and angelica is an easy herb to grow), do have a go at candying some yourself. They will be far superior to their shop-bought alternative – less startling in colour, perhaps, but rich with angelica's unique aromatic, slightly astringent flavour. Also look out for the bright young leaves of alexanders, which flourish along roadsides during spring and early summer. The stems of these seaside-loving plants, as John Wright suggests in his *Edible Seashore* handbook, make a delicious addition to cakes. This is John's recipe to candy alexanders, which I've appropriated for angelica.

Choose young, tender springtime shoots and trim to roughly 10cm lengths. Place them in a saucepan with just enough water to cover and simmer until softened. Remove from the heat and allow to cool a little. Remove the angelica with a slotted spoon, reserving the water, and trim away any tough outer fibres. Weigh the stems, then add the same weight of sugar to the pan of cooking water. Dissolve over a medium heat and bring to the boil. Lay the angelica stems in a flat dish and pour over the sugar syrup. Cover and leave for a day.

Pour the syrup back into the pan and bring to the boil. Simmer for a few minutes to reduce slightly, then pour back over the angelica and leave for another day.

Repeat the process for another 2 days, then drain off the remaining syrup and lay the angelica stems on wire racks. Either dry them in a low oven at 40–50°C for 4 hours or in a warm, dry place over several days. Store, when completely dry, wrapped in greaseproof paper in a sealed jam jar or airtight container.

Small Cakes & Bakes

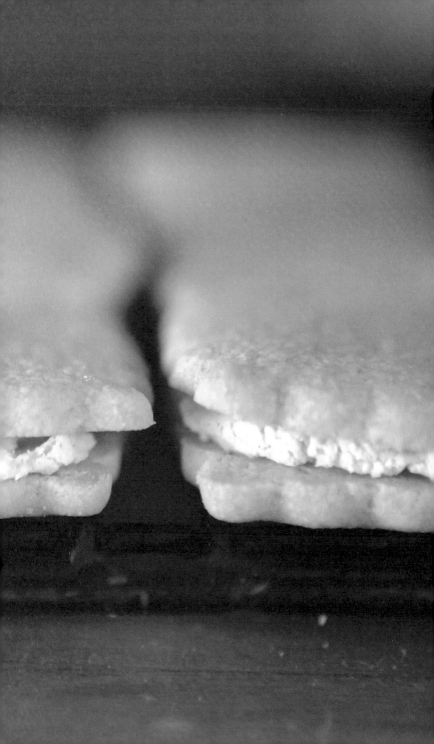

The little gems in this chapter break down into three categories. First there are the utilitarian ones, quick to fix and great hunger stoppers – the unleavened kind that are typical of the earliest of 'cakes'. These recipes are the sort you get to know by heart and can effortlessly knock up in a few minutes or so, brilliant to bake as your guests arrive at the door. They include the down-to-earth, swift-to-make Welsh cakes – cooked on a hot griddle in no more than 6 minutes – and the ever-popular energy-packed bars like flapjacks. Incidentally, the cakes King Alfred burnt were most likely the forerunners of Welsh cakes.

Then there are the everyday specials – crisp biscuits warmly flavoured with lively spices and soft-centred cookies to bake off whenever the desire arises. Not forgetting the timeless classic of the Scottish larder, shortbread – once perfected, this will give you a baking reputation second to none. However, here lies a word of warning from a voice of experience. If you enter the shortbread class at your local show, bear in mind that judging at these village affairs can be very subjective. If, for some reason, your entry does not win, graciously accept the miscarriage of justice and don't worry about it. Well, at least not until the following year.

The ultimates in this section are the heartbreakers, the adorables, the enticers – the little devils that destroy all your willpower by their persuasive sumptuousness: sweet chewy macaroons, salt caramel shortbread, the unctuous and universally popular chocolate brownie. The members of this elite and somewhat flamboyant set are unquestionably best reserved for special times when you will need to exercise a certain amount of restraint if you are to have just the one portion and no more. Even in their making, you'll be giddy with excitement and anticipation, knowing the best moment is yet to come.

Welsh cakes

These little icons of the Welsh table – *Teisen lap* – are as symbolic of their country as the leek and daffodil. Similar to a scone, they are often referred to as 'bakestones', which harks back to times past when baking was done on a hot hearth or flagstone. These days, a good heavy-based frying pan will suffice. Welsh cakes are delicious just as they are, or spread with butter and perhaps a little jam. Then again, a couple of leeks and a little cheese will turn them into a savoury teatime treat.

Makes 12

250g self-raising flour
½ tsp sea salt
100g unsalted butter, cut into
    small cubes

100g caster sugar, plus 1 tbsp to finish
100g currants
1 egg, beaten
1 tbsp milk, plus a bit extra if needed

Sift the flour and salt into a large bowl. With your fingertips, lightly rub in the butter until the mixture resembles fine breadcrumbs, then add the caster sugar and currants. Mix in the beaten egg and bring the mixture together with a fork to form a soft dough, adding as much milk as you need to do so.

Turn onto a floured surface and use your palm or a rolling pin to pat or roll out to a 6–7mm thickness. Using a scone cutter or upturned glass, cut out 6–7cm circles.

Heat an ungreased griddle or frying pan over a medium heat. It needs to be hot, but not so hot that it will blacken the cakes. Drop the cakes onto the hot surface and cook one side before turning over to cook the other. The rule of thumb is to cook for about 3 minutes on each side until a lovely medium caramel colour. If they are browning more quickly than this, your griddle is probably too hot.

Transfer the cakes to a wire rack and leave to cool. Before serving, sprinkle with a little caster sugar.

Variations

Honey (*Teisen mel*) Replace the sugar with 2 level tbsp honey and add the grated zest of an unwaxed lemon or an orange.

Mincemeat (*Teisen briwgig*) Omit the milk and add 3–4 tbsp mincemeat to the mixture. Use a star cutter to shape festive cakes.

Leek and cheese (*Teisen cennin*) Soften 100g finely sliced leeks in a little butter, cool and add to the dough with 50g grated Cheddar or Caerphilly cheese.

Flapjacks

Soft and chewy or crisp and crunchy, as you prefer, flapjacks are one of the all-time greats – lunchtime or teatime, a good flapjack is difficult to beat. They are really easy to make; indeed they were the first things I ever baked as a child. This well-used recipe is easily adapted to make a flapjack to please everyone.

Now when it comes to your oats, perhaps surprisingly, biggest isn't the best. Medium-sized (normal) porridge oats stick together much better than jumbo oats.

Makes 12–16

175g unsalted butter, cut into cubes
1 tbsp golden syrup
150g demerara sugar
250g medium porridge oats
Pinch of sea salt
1 tbsp desiccated coconut (optional)

Equipment
25 x 20cm shallow baking tin, lightly greased and base-lined with baking parchment

Preheat the oven to 180°C/Gas mark 4. Place the butter, golden syrup and sugar in a large heavy-based saucepan. Heat gently, stirring often, until the butter has just melted and the sugar is still grainy. Remove from the heat and pour in the porridge oats, salt and desiccated coconut, if using. Mix together until evenly combined.

Turn the mixture into the prepared baking tray, spread evenly and firm down well with a fork or the back of a spoon. For a soft and chewy flapjack, bake for about 20 minutes until a light-medium golden colour. Give it a bit longer if you prefer a crispy, well-cooked flapjack.

Run a knife round the edge to release the flapjack, leave for 5 minutes, then mark into bars or squares. Leave in the tin until nearly cold before cutting into pieces and removing to a wire rack. The flapjacks will keep in an airtight tin for up to 10 days.

Variations

Raisin and honey Omit the coconut and golden syrup. Replace with 2 level tbsp honey (about 50g), 100g raisins and the grated zest of 1 unwaxed orange.

Muesli Replace the oats with 300g of your favourite muesli.

Cherry and coconut Add 50g desiccated coconut and 75g quartered glacé cherries.

Walnut and maple syrup Omit the desiccated coconut, replace the golden syrup with 1–2 tbsp maple syrup and add 75g chopped walnuts.

Fruit, nut and honey bars

Judging by the number of different 'energy bars' on the market these days, we all ought to be bursting with vitality and *joie de vivre*. You'll find these sweet snacks, breakfast bars and filler-uppers just about everywhere – at railway stations for munching on long lonely journeys and at health food shops and supermarkets. Many of them are tempting, but some are little more than sugar and additives. Nevertheless, the idea of an energy-dense, sustaining, compact mini meal that's easy to eat on the move is certainly a good one. This is my take on the theme: packed with loads of fruit, nuts and seeds, these natural snack bars are easy to make, nutritious and much cheaper than shop-bought alternatives.

Makes 15–16

125g unsalted butter, cut into cubes
100g light soft brown or demerara
    sugar
100g honey
150ml fresh apple or orange juice
Finely grated zest of 1 orange
200g porridge oats (or 150g oats plus
    50g puffed rice or wheat flakes)
100g dried dates, chopped
100g dried apricots, chopped
50g chopped walnuts, hazelnuts
    or almonds
125g mixed seeds such as pumpkin,
    linseed, poppy, sunflower

Equipment
18 x 25cm or 20cm square shallow
    baking tin, lightly greased and
    base-lined with baking parchment

Preheat the oven to 180°C/Gas mark 4. Put the butter, sugar, honey, fruit juice and orange zest into a large saucepan over a low heat and stir from time to time until the butter has melted and the ingredients are blended together. Remove from the heat, add the oats, puffed rice or wheat if using, dried dates and apricots, nuts and 100g of the mixed seeds. Stir well.

Transfer the mixture to the prepared baking tin and level the surface with the back of the spoon. Sprinkle the remaining seeds evenly over the top. Bake in the oven for 25–30 minutes until golden brown on top.

Leave in the tin to cool before turning out and cutting into squares or fingers with a sharp knife. They will keep for 10 days stored in an airtight tin.

Rock cakes

Hard or soft, igneous or indigenous, rock cakes are archetypal of church fêtes and school bazaars. Often and unfairly outdone by the more louche and luscious-looking chocolate brownie, they're the plain Janes of the station buffet. But don't judge a book by its cover – freshly made rock cakes are quite delightful. Their name derives not from their texture but from their rather craggy appearance; they should not be *rock* hard, but soft and crumbly inside with a golden baked exterior. Using everyday store-cupboard ingredients, they are quick and easy to make, ideal for impromptu picnics and unexpected teatime visitors.

Makes 8

100g self-raising white flour
100g self-raising wholemeal flour
Pinch of sea salt
100g unsalted butter, cut into
    small pieces
75g light soft brown sugar

175g raisins
Finely grated zest of 1 unwaxed orange
1 large egg, beaten

Equipment
Large baking sheet, lightly greased

Preheat the oven to 190°C/Gas mark 5. Sift the flours and salt into a mixing bowl. Add the butter and lightly rub into the flour, using your fingertips, until the mixture resembles fine, even breadcrumbs. Mix in the brown sugar, raisins and orange zest, tossing together until evenly mixed.

Add the beaten egg and use a fork to bring the mix together into a soft, crumbly dough. It may be necessary to knead a little by hand but keep the dough light and open-textured so it can form some good outcrops.

Divide the mixture into 8 pieces, shape into irregular balls and place well apart on the greased baking sheet. Bake for 15–20 minutes, until golden and firm to the touch. Leave for 5–10 minutes before removing with a palette knife to a wire rack to cool.

Rock cakes will keep for up to 3 days in an airtight container but they are definitely best eaten fresh.

Variations

Currant and lemon Replace the raisins and orange with currants and lemon zest.

Spelt, date, apricot and ginger Replace the flours with spelt or wholemeal flour and the raisins with 75g chopped dates, 75g chopped apricots and 50g chopped preserved stem ginger, drained of its syrup.

Anzac biscuits

This recipe from Down Under is a poignant reminder of the hardships the Forces endured during World War I. Wives, lovers and mothers would make these oaty biscuits to send to Anzac (Australian and New Zealand Army Corps) troops fighting thousands of miles away at Gallipoli in Turkey. There was no refrigeration on the ships, so the biscuits required a good shelf (or ship) life to ensure they didn't go off during the two-month voyage.

Makes 12

125g plain flour
100g medium oatmeal or
   porridge oats
100g light soft brown sugar
50g desiccated coconut
100g unsalted butter, cut into cubes
1 tbsp golden syrup or honey
½ tsp bicarbonate of soda
1 tbsp boiling water

Equipment
Large baking sheet, lightly greased or
   lined with baking parchment

Preheat the oven to 170°C/Gas mark 3. Sift the flour into a medium mixing bowl. Add the oatmeal, brown sugar and coconut and mix together thoroughly.

Put the butter and golden syrup or honey into a small saucepan. Place over a low heat until the butter has melted. Meanwhile, put the bicarbonate of soda into a cup and pour on the boiling water to dissolve.

Next, stir the bicarbonate of soda mix into the melted butter; be very careful – the mixture will rapidly fizz and foam up. Pour the frothing mixture into the dry ingredients. Using a wooden spoon, quickly mix together to form a thick batter.

Place generous tablespoonfuls of the mixture onto the prepared baking sheet, allowing room for spreading. Gently flatten the tops with the back of a fork. Bake for about 20 minutes until golden brown.

Leave the biscuits on the baking sheet for 10 minutes to firm up before transferring to a wire rack to cool. Stored in an airtight tin, they will keep for up to 3 months.

Variation

If you have any stale cornflakes that need using up, lightly crush 75g of these and use instead of the oatmeal.

Shortbread

Originally I thought that this would be a short recipe. However, the more I bake this member of the biscuit clan, the more I realise that to make tender melt-in-the-mouth shortbread, you need to understand a few hard-and-fast rules.

Shortbread relies on really good-quality unsalted butter for its flavour, so don't skimp on this and never use margarine! The high butter (or 'shortening') content helps to keep the gluten in the flour short and soft. But, for that delectable, friable texture, it's also important to keep a light hand. Overworking the mixture will make the dough oily; it will also develop the gluten in the flour and make the shortbread tough.

You need to choose your flour carefully. Most recipes call for a 2:1 mix of plain wheat flour and rice flour or cornflour, for a very soft texture, but you can also use semolina for a slightly crunchier result. Sifting in the flour is a valuable step that helps to keep the shortbread light and melting.

And the final crucial thing to remember is that shortbread must be only barely coloured, never browned. So, don't forget it's in the oven...

Makes about 15

150g unsalted butter, cut into
   small pieces, softened
75g caster sugar (I like to use vanilla
   sugar), plus extra for dredging
150g plain flour
75g rice flour

Equipment
2 baking sheets, lined with baking
   parchment, or a 20cm loose-based
   fluted flan tin or plain sandwich tin

Preheat the oven to 170°C/Gas mark 3. Put the softened butter into a bowl. Using a wooden spoon, gradually work in the sugar until it is well mixed and forms a soft paste. Sift in the flour and rice flour. Using a fork, bring together lightly to form a soft, crumbly dough. It's hands-on (or in) time now: bring the mix to a soft, pliable, crack-free dough by kneading it as lightly as possible.

For biscuits, place the dough between two sheets of lightly floured greaseproof paper. Using a rolling pin, roll out to a 5mm thickness. Remove the top paper and cut out biscuits using a 6–7cm fluted cutter or a shaped biscuit cutter (heart, star, leaf, etc.). Place the biscuits on the baking sheets and prick the surface with a fork.

For a shortbread round, lightly press the dough into the loose-based 20cm flan tin or sandwich tin, or shape into a round, about 2cm thick, by hand. To finish the edge, pinch into little flutes with your thumb and finger. Prick the surface with a fork.

Bake the shortbread in the oven until very lightly coloured; allow about 20 minutes for biscuits, 30–35 minutes for a shortbread round. Dredge with sugar and place on a wire rack to cool. Shortbread will keep for up to 4 weeks in an airtight tin.

Variations

Hazelnut shortbread Replace the caster with light soft brown sugar and the rice flour with 75g ground hazelnuts.

Lovers' shortbread Add 2–3 tsp rose water with the sifted flour. Use a heart-shaped biscuit cutter.

Thyme shortbread Add 1 tbsp finely chopped thyme. This is lovely with summer sorbets, ices and fruits.

Lancashire (Goosenargh) shortbread Add 1 tsp caraway seeds and ½ tsp ground coriander powder with the flour.

Chocolate-dipped shortbread Melt 100g chocolate in a bowl over a pan of hot water. Dip one half of each shortbread biscuit in the chocolate to partially coat. Place on baking parchment to dry.

Strawberry shortbread Cover a shortbread round with whipped double cream and top with fresh strawberries (or raspberries).

Jammy dodgers

Some might say that life is too short to bake homemade versions of biscuit tin favourites. However, I think you might find these homages to some of our favourite sweet treats will become the revered jewels of your tea table. They will delight everyone, bring a smile or two (because they normally come in packets) and turn a simple tea into a ritzy, classy occasion.

Makes 6 or 7

175g plain flour
Pinch of sea salt
75g unrefined icing sugar
125g unsalted butter, cut into
   small pieces
1 egg yolk
1 tsp vanilla extract
150g raspberry jam (or whatever
   flavour you like)

Equipment
2 large baking sheets, lined with
   baking parchment
6–7cm biscuit cutter, crinkle-edged
   or plain
2.5cm heart, square, round or animal
   biscuit cutter, crinkle-edged
   or plain

Sift the flour, salt and icing sugar into a large mixing bowl. Add the butter and lightly rub into the flour mix, using your fingertips, until the mixture resembles fine breadcrumbs.

In a small bowl, whisk the egg yolk and vanilla extract together. Make a well in the centre of the flour mix. Add the egg and vanilla mix and work together to form a soft, smooth dough. Alternatively, you can simply place everything in a food processor and bring to this stage. Seal the dough in a polythene bag and chill in the fridge for 25–30 minutes.

Preheat the oven to 170°C/Gas mark 3. Divide the dough into two equal portions. Place one portion between two pieces of lightly floured greaseproof paper and, using a rolling pin, roll the dough to approximately a 4mm thickness. Repeat with the second piece of dough. Remove the top paper.

With the larger biscuit cutter, cut the dough into discs (make sure you have an even number). Using the smaller cutter, cut out and remove the centre of half the biscuit discs; the cut-out pieces can either be kneaded back into the remaining dough or baked just as they are.

Place all the discs on the baking sheets. Bake for 15–20 minutes until just firm and barely coloured.

Remove from the oven and place a teaspoonful of jam in the centre of each whole biscuit round. Spread to 1.5cm from the edge. Place the cut-out rounds on top. Return to the oven and cook for a further 5–6 minutes by which time the biscuits will be evenly cooked and the jam sufficiently hot to stick the biscuits together.

Leave the biscuits to cool for 5 minutes before transferring to a wire cooling rack.

Variations

Custard creams Replace 50g of the flour with custard powder. Use a 5cm square biscuit cutter. Bake the biscuits for about 20 minutes until lightly coloured. Cool on a wire rack. To make the custard cream filling, simply cream together 75g softened unsalted butter, 75g icing sugar and 25g custard powder. To finish, sandwich the cooled biscuits together in pairs with a teaspoonful of the filling. *Makes 14*

Bourbon biscuits Replace 50g of the flour with drinking chocolate powder or, for a dark rich biscuit, use cocoa powder. Use an oblong biscuit cutter, about 6–7 x 2.5cm. With a fork, lightly prick the surface of the uncooked biscuits (just like the packet ones). Bake for approximately 20 minutes. To make the chocolate cream filling, cream together 75g softened unsalted butter, 75g icing sugar and 25g drinking chocolate or cocoa powder. To finish, sandwich the cooled biscuits together in pairs with a teaspoonful of the filling. *Makes 12*

Christmas tree biscuits

For me, one of the highlights in the lead-up to Christmas is a happy few hours spent at my friend Henriette's house, making biscuits for the festive season. It's an afternoon of free choice, when tree-shaped biscuits sometimes turn pink and sugared sheep can end up with multi-coloured fleeces. This is the recipe I always use – it produces lovely, crunchy, warmly spiced biscuits. They are by no means exclusively for Christmas, by the way. You can use the recipe to make 'run, run, as fast as you can' gingerbread men too (see overleaf).

*Makes about 24 (depending
    on size of cutters)*
275g plain flour
1 level tsp baking powder
1 tsp ground ginger
1 tsp ground cinnamon
100g soft brown sugar
75g unsalted butter, cut into
    small pieces
1 egg, lightly beaten
50g golden syrup

Equipment
2 baking sheets, lightly greased or
    lined with baking parchment
Christmas biscuit cutters (trees, stars,
    holly leaves, etc.)

To decorate
Glacé icing (see p.55)
2 or 3 natural food colourings (see p.56)
Cherries, angelica, currants, desiccated
    coconut, flaked almonds, walnuts,
    sesame seeds, chocolate or coloured
    sprinkles, sugar, etc.

Preheat the oven to 170°C/Gas mark 3. Sift the flour, baking powder and spices into a mixing bowl. Add the brown sugar and mix well. Add the butter and rub in with your fingertips until the mixture resembles fine breadcrumbs.

In another bowl, mix the egg and golden syrup together until smooth and well blended. Make a well in the centre of the rubbed-in mixture and pour in the egg and syrup. Using a wooden spoon, mix together to form a ball of dough.

Put the dough into a polythene bag and place in the fridge for 30 minutes to rest; this will make it much easier to roll out.

(continued overleaf)

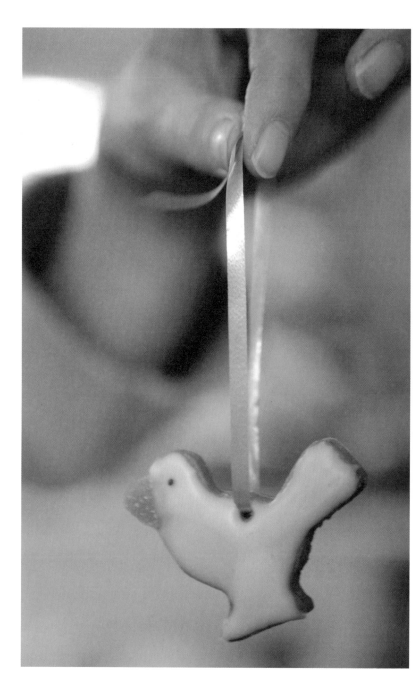

When you are ready to bake the biscuits, place the dough between two lightly floured sheets of greaseproof paper. Roll the dough out evenly until it is approximately 5mm thick, then remove the top paper. Cut out shapes from the dough with your chosen biscuit cutters.

Place the biscuits on the baking sheets, leaving space in between for them to spread a little. Use a knitting needle or skewer to make a hole near the top of each shape (this is to thread a hanging ribbon through).

Bake for 15–20 minutes until the biscuits are golden brown. They will still seem soft at this stage, but will firm up as they cool. If necessary, re-make the holes while they are still hot. Transfer to a wire rack to cool.

When ready to finish, divide the white glacé icing between three or four small bowls. Keep one bowl white and colour the others as desired. Using either the back of a spoon or a small round-ended knife, carefully spread plain or coloured glacé icing over one side of each biscuit (to get a really smooth finish, dip the spoon or knife in a jug of just-boiled water first). Add decorations of your choice. Lay the biscuits on a wire rack and leave until the icing has set.

Finally, thread the biscuits with ribbon or raffia and hang on the Christmas tree. For utmost effect, hang a few biscuits on the tree every couple of days. Alternatively, and to last for the full festive period, wrap the biscuits in cellophane before hanging.

These biscuits will keep un-iced for 3 months in an airtight tin.

Variation

Gingerbread men Use a traditional 'gingerbread man' biscuit cutter. To give the biscuits their endearing personalities, before baking add currants for eyes, sliced cherries for lips and dried cranberries/diced dried apricots for shirt buttons. For gingerbread girls, use a jumble of finely cut dried fruits to create skirts to skip in. Alternatively, leave the biscuits plain and then ice and titivate with coloured chocolate buttons, etc., after baking and cooling.

Dog bone biscuits

I do think it's important to keep everyone in the family happy. These are designed as very special treats for dogs, but there's nothing in them that would bar anyone else from taking a chew.

Makes about 24 large bones or
100 little ones
250g wholemeal flour
125g fine oatmeal
125g porridge oats
150ml sunflower or rapeseed oil
2 eggs, lightly beaten
200g carrots, trimmed and finely grated (only peel if dirty)
2 tsp caraway seeds
2 tbsp finely chopped parsley

Equipment
2 large baking sheets, lined with baking parchment
Dog bone biscuit cutter, about 12x3cm (or a smaller one)

Preheat the oven to 170°C/Gas mark 3. Sift the flour into a mixing bowl. Add the oatmeal and porridge oats and mix together. Make a well in the centre and pour in the oil, followed by the beaten eggs, carrots, caraway seeds and parsley. Mix with a wooden spoon until well blended and you have a fairly sticky dough.

Lightly dust the work surface with flour, then turn out the dough and knead for a few minutes until the mixture is smooth and pliable.

Place the dough between two sheets of lightly floured greaseproof paper. Using a rolling pin, roll the dough out to about a 5mm thickness and remove the top paper. Cut out biscuits using the bone cutter and place on the prepared baking sheets.

Bake in the oven for about 50 minutes or until the biscuits are crisp and lightly golden. Cool on a wire rack. These will keep for 2 months in an airtight container.

Variation

Courgette and ginger Replace the carrots with courgettes, the caraway seeds with ginger and the parsley with coriander.

P.S. For 'human' dog bone biscuits, use the recipe for Jammy dodgers (see p.84) or the one for Christmas tree biscuits (see p.86), but cut out with the bone cutter. Coat with Glacé icing (see p.55) and decorate with chocolate buttons, sugar sprinkles, glacé cherries or nuts, though you may find the family prefer the dog's bones!

'Bake-off' cookies

Lightly crisp on the outside, meltingly soft inside, who doesn't love cookies straight from the oven? Keep a roll of cookie dough in the fridge (for up to a week), and you can enjoy these freshly baked treats any time. Alternatively, the dough can be sliced and frozen, allowing you to 'bake off' any number at a time. Freeze on a tray before packing into a sealed bag; allow to defrost for 15 minutes before baking.

Makes 18

225g unsalted butter, softened
225g caster sugar
1 egg yolk
250g plain flour
½ tsp baking powder
Pinch of sea salt

100g plain chocolate, roughly
   chopped into 1cm pieces
50g hazelnuts, roughly chopped

Equipment
2 baking sheets, lightly greased or
   lined with baking parchment

Beat the butter and sugar together in a mixing bowl until light and creamy, then mix in the egg yolk. Sift in the flour, baking powder and salt. Using a fork, bring together to a soft dough. Carefully mix in the chocolate and nuts until evenly distributed.

Lightly dust a piece of greaseproof paper with flour and turn the dough onto it. Shape into a cylinder, about 7cm in diameter and 20cm long, and wrap securely in the paper. Place in the fridge for about an hour to firm up.

When ready to cook, preheat the oven to 170°C/Gas mark 3. Remove the dough from the fridge and cut into slices, 1–1.5cm thick, using a sharp knife. Place on the baking sheets, leaving plenty of space for the cookies to spread.

Bake for 20–25 minutes until the cookies are just turning golden brown at the edges. Use a palette knife to transfer them to a wire rack and leave to cool.

These cookies will keep in an airtight container for up to 2 days.

Variations

Classic chocolate chip Omit the hazelnuts and increase the chocolate to 200g. (You can use plain, milk or white chocolate.)

Oatmeal and raisin Replace 100g of the flour with oatmeal or porridge oats. Omit the chocolate and nuts. Add 150g Lexia raisins and the zest of 1 unwaxed orange.

Ginger Replace the chocolate and nuts with 125g roughly chopped stem ginger.

Cornish fairings

A close cousin of the gingernut, the Cornish fairing is a spicy, crisp gingery biscuit, nutty brown in colour and deeply cracked. The name originates from early lively trading and festival fairs, where the biscuits were bought by visitors as gifts or 'fairings' to take home. This recipe, by far the best I've found, comes from Jo, one of our lady Cornish pilot gig rowers in Lyme Regis.

Makes 6 large fairings
125g plain flour
1 tsp baking powder
½ tsp bicarbonate of soda
1 good tsp ground ginger
1 tsp ground mixed spice
50g caster sugar
50g unsalted butter, cut into
    small pieces
2 tbsp golden syrup

Equipment
**Baking sheet, lightly greased or
    lined with baking parchment**

Preheat the oven to 200°C/Gas mark 6. Sift the first five ingredients into a large bowl and stir in the caster sugar. Add the butter and, using your fingertips, lightly rub it in until the mixture resembles fine breadcrumbs. Add the golden syrup and use a fork to bring the mixture together to a soft dough. Alternatively, simply place all the ingredients in a food processor and whiz until mixed to a smooth dough.

Divide the dough into 6 pieces. With floured hands, roll each into a ball about the size of a very large walnut. Place on the baking sheet, allowing plenty of room for spreading. Keeping them round, flatten slightly with the back of a fork.

Bake in the oven for 7–8 minutes, until nutty golden brown in colour and deeply cracked on the surface. Stay around and don't get too engrossed on the phone – a minute or two too long and you'll have half a dozen frisbees instead of fairings.

Leave to firm up on the baking sheet for a couple of minutes before transferring to a wire cooling rack. Once cool, these will keep for a week or so in an airtight tin.

P.S. Golden syrup is tricky to measure accurately. The easiest way is to place a metal measuring spoon in a cup of very hot water prior to measuring out the syrup. The heat makes the syrup slip off the spoon neatly and cleanly and should give you a fairly true measure.

Butterfly and fairy cakes

So simple to make, these feather-light party favourites will please young and old alike. A nick with a knife transforms the basic fairy cake into a fluttering butterfly cake. Straightforward iced cup cakes can be made from this recipe too: just flood the surface with plain or flavoured Glacé icing (see p.55) or Buttercream (see p.49) and titivate with decorations of your choice.

Makes 12 or 24 (depending on tray)

175g self-raising flour
1 tsp baking powder
125g caster sugar
125g unsalted butter, softened and
    cut into small pieces
2 eggs
1 tsp vanilla extract (optional)

Equipment
12-hole muffin tray, holes about
    6.5cm in diameter and 2cm deep,
    lightly greased or lined with
    paper muffin cases, or 2 x 12-hole
    bun tins, lined with small paper
    cake cases

To finish
1 quantity Vanilla buttercream
    (see p.49)
Icing sugar to dredge

Preheat the oven to 190°C/Gas mark 5. Sift the flour and baking powder into a large mixing bowl. Add the sugar and beat for a few seconds until well blended. Add the butter, eggs, vanilla extract, if using, and 1 tbsp hot water. Using an electric whisk, beat until smooth; this should take no more than 1½–2 minutes.

Carefully spoon the mixture into the paper cases so they are about two-thirds full. Give the baking tray a couple of sharp taps on the work surface to level the mixture in the cases.

Bake in the oven until well risen and golden; allow 12–14 minutes for smaller cakes and an extra couple of minutes for bigger cakes. Leave in the trays for 5 minutes before moving to a wire rack and leaving to cool completely.

Once the cakes have cooled, you can simply top them with the vanilla buttercream to make fairy cakes.

Alternatively, to make butterfly cakes, use a small sharp knife to cut a circle from the top of each cake, leaving a border of about 1cm. Remove the cone-shaped centre, leaving a slight hollow. Cut the removed cones in half to make the butterfly wings and set aside (no nibbling, butterflies need two wings). Put 1 tsp buttercream into the hollow of each cake. Press the wings, cut side uppermost, into the icing and sift over a little icing sugar to finish. These will keep for 5 days in an airtight tin.

Variations

Change the look and taste of butterfly cakes by placing a fresh raspberry or strawberry between the wings or dropping a little jam in the centre before topping with the buttercream. Or use chocolate buttercream and top with chocolate buttons.

'Veg patch' gnome cakes

These fab (and fatless) relatives of the fairy cake are a brilliant way to use up surplus produce from the veg patch. They are also perfect for enticing young reluctant veg eaters. Camouflaged in a sweet cake mix, you'll find grated pumpkin, parsnips, carrots and courgettes disappear without a murmur of dissent...

Makes 12 large cup cakes
200g self-raising flour
1 tsp baking powder
Pinch of sea salt
3 eggs
175g caster sugar
200g uncooked, finely grated
     pumpkin
Finely grated zest of 1 unwaxed
     orange

For the icing
1 quantity Cream cheese topping
     flavoured with orange zest (see p.57)

To decorate
Edible flowers (borage, marigolds,
     fennel), Marzipan vegetables
     (see p.59), or other decorations
     of your choice

Equipment
12-hole muffin tray, holes about
     6.5cm in diameter and 2cm deep,
     lightly greased or lined with
     paper muffin cases, or 2 x 12-hole
     bun tins, lined with small paper
     cake cases

Preheat the oven to 180°C/Gas mark 4. Sift the flour with the baking powder and salt. Beat the eggs and sugar together in a large bowl with a hand-held electric whisk for 5–6 minutes until the mixture is thick, creamy and pale. Fold in the flour, half at a time, using a large metal spoon. Finally fold in the pumpkin and orange zest.

Carefully spoon the mixture into the paper cases so they are three-quarters full. Bake for about 20 minutes or until lightly golden and springy to the touch. Leave in the trays for about 5 minutes, then transfer to a wire rack to cool.

When cool, top with the cream cheese topping and add decorations of your choice. These will keep for 2–3 days in an airtight tin.

Variations
Carrot gnome Replace the pumpkin with carrot and the orange zest with lemon.

Parsnip gnome Replace the pumpkin with parsnip and the orange zest with lime.

Courgette gnome Replace the pumpkin with courgette, the orange zest with lemon and add ½ tsp freshly grated nutmeg.

Muffins (American-style)

Making voluminous, blowsy, puffed-up muffins – with bags more tops than bottoms – is simplicity itself. Once you've got the hang of it, you'll have great fun dreaming up your own variations, flavoured with perfectly partnered ingredients. Make your muffins sweet or savoury, for breakfast, lunch or tea. You'll also find them a thrifty way to use up odds and ends discovered during a fridge clear-out. There are a couple of rules for success but, once you've learnt them, you'll soon find yourself turning out batches of whopping big muffins in minutes.

I could practically fill a book with muffin recipes alone – the basic recipe is so endlessly adaptable. Before you begin experimenting with flavouring ingredients, you can play around with the main ones.

Flour Use a plain flour of your choice: either white, wholemeal, spelt or a 50/50 mix of any of these. Alternatively, you can make gluten-free muffins with a pre-mixed gluten-free self-raising cake flour, such as those made by Doves Farm or Bia Nua (see directory, p.244). Add ½ tsp each of baking powder and bicarbonate of soda per batch of muffins or 250g flour.

Sugar Caster is the classic choice, but you can switch it for soft brown or muscovado. Alternatively, sweeten your muffins with honey, golden syrup or molasses, replacing the caster sugar with about three-quarters of the amount. Add more, or less, to suit the muffin and please the palate.

Milk/yoghurt You can use full-fat or semi-skimmed milk. Try goat's milk as an alternative – or soya milk and soya yoghurt for dairy-free muffins. You can also replace the yoghurt with buttermilk or soured cream.

Fat/oil Butter, which needs to be melted then cooled, is most often used in muffins, but I also like to use sunflower or rapeseed oil or a mixture of both.

The golden rules of muffin-making:
Ingredients are divided into wet and dry. The dry ingredients (i.e. flour, raising agents, spices, etc.) are sifted into a mixing bowl, combined with the sugar and blended thoroughly. Ideally, and to save on the washing up, you can then put all the wet ingredients into a measuring jug (angled if possible), along with any herbs or essences, and beat until thoroughly combined.

The mixing method contrasts with many other cake-making techniques in that it does not involve vigorous beating or whisking. Instead, a large metal spoon or flexible spatula is used to mix the combined wet ingredients swiftly and lightly into the dry ones, forming a lumpy batter. *Do not* beat to a super-smooth batter or you will find yourself with dense, heavy muffins.

The batter can be put straight into the well-greased cups of a muffin tray, or paper muffin cases can be used to line the cups – for big muffin tops, use paper cases about 3cm high, rather than deep ones. But the way I like to cook my muffins is to line the cups with baking parchment squares, roughly 15cm square. Don't try to line the whole muffin tray before filling, just line as you fill. The squares are easiest to mould into the cups if they are first folded in half diagonally and opened as you fill. For full-blown muffin tops, three-quarter fill the cups with the muffin batter.

Bake the muffins in the centre of a fairly hot oven (200°C/Gas mark 6) for 20–25 minutes until very well risen and domed. They should spring back into shape when lightly touched with a finger. Leave in the tray for a few minutes, then transfer to a wire rack to cool a little before eating.

Muffins don't keep well and are best eaten fresh from the oven or within 24 hours of baking. However, they do freeze very well if frozen on the day of baking.

And now for the recipes:

I've given three types of muffin over the following pages: a substantial breakfast one; a delectable savoury affair; and a sweet, fruity muffin. In each case, I've suggested lots of variations and I hope you'll add your own...

Banana breakfast muffins

Generally, even the sparrows turn their beaks up at cold leftover porridge. But this resourceful recipe is a great way to use up the cup or so of glutinous stuff that often remains at the bottom of the porridge pan. Prepare the wet and dry ingredients the night before and you can quickly turn leftover porridge into a rather splendid way to start the following day.

Makes 10 large muffins
225g plain flour
2 tsp baking powder
½ tsp bicarbonate of soda
½ tsp sea salt
1–2 tsp ground cinnamon
100g light muscovado sugar, plus
    extra for sprinkling
100ml plain yoghurt
30–50ml milk
1 egg
100ml sunflower or rapeseed oil
150g cold cooked porridge
2 ripe bananas, 1 mashed to a purée,
    1 sliced into 10 pieces

Equipment
12-hole muffin tray, holes about
    6.5cm in diameter and 2cm deep,
    10 lightly greased or lined with
    10 paper muffin cases or 15cm
    baking parchment squares

Preheat the oven to 200°C/Gas mark 6. Sift the first five ingredients into a medium mixing bowl. Add the sugar and mix together evenly, either by mixing with a spoon or beating with an electric mixer for about 30 seconds on the lowest speed.

Next put the measured yoghurt, 30ml milk, egg, oil, porridge and the mashed banana into a large mixing jug or bowl. Beat together until well combined and the mixture is like a very thick batter, adding extra milk if it is too thick. Pour into the dry ingredients and stir very lightly, scraping the sides down, until *just* combined, with no clumps of dry flour lurking in the bottom of the mixing bowl.

Divide the mixture between the muffin cups, filling each to three-quarters full (this will be about one fully laden tablespoonful per cup). Pop a piece of banana in the centre of each and sprinkle with a little muscovado sugar.

Bake in the oven for 20–25 minutes until well risen and the tops are golden. The muffins should spring back into shape when lightly touched.

Breakfast muffin variations

Follow the simple method of combining the dry ingredients, combining the wet ingredients, then mixing lightly together.

Marmalade For the dry ingredients, use 250g plain flour, 2 tsp baking powder, ½ tsp bicarbonate of soda, ½ tsp sea salt, ½ tsp ground ginger or 1 tsp ground cardamom and 100g light muscovado sugar. For the wet ingredients, use 125ml milk, 125ml plain yoghurt, 1 egg, 100ml sunflower oil and 150g marmalade. Sprinkle with 1 tbsp muscovado sugar to finish.

Smoked salmon and eggs For the dry ingredients, use 250g plain flour, 2 tsp baking powder, ½ tsp bicarbonate of soda, ½ tsp sea salt and ½ tsp cayenne pepper. For the wet ingredients, use 125ml milk, 125ml soured cream, 2 eggs, 100ml sunflower oil, 125g smoked salmon pieces and 1 tbsp chopped chives.

Mopping-up muffins for bacon and egg breakfast juices For the dry ingredients, use 125g cornflour, 125g wholemeal flour, 75g light muscovado sugar, 2 tsp baking powder, ½ tsp bicarbonate of soda and ½ tsp sea salt. For the wet ingredients, use 125ml milk and 125ml plain yoghurt (or just 250ml milk), 1 egg and 100ml sunflower or rapeseed oil.

Wild garlic and cheese muffins

I have more fun dreaming up mouthwatering ideas for savoury muffins than any others. Baked for elevenses or lunchtime, these are a delight to make and utterly delicious to eat. Wild garlic appears from the middle of March until the second or third week of May. Its heady, yet sweet aroma combines beautifully with strong, flavoursome Cheddar to make moreishly good muffins. Replace the wild garlic with fresh garden herbs when the season is over, or use 1–2 tbsp pesto instead.

Makes 10 large muffins

250g plain flour
2 tsp baking powder
½ tsp bicarbonate of soda
½ tsp sea salt
1 tsp English mustard powder or
    ½ tsp cayenne powder (optional)
125ml milk
125ml plain yoghurt
1 egg
100ml sunflower or rapeseed oil
2 level tbsp finely chopped wild garlic
    leaves (about 20 leaves)

100–150g strong Cheddar cheese,
    finely grated
5 cherry tomatoes, halved

Equipment
12-hole muffin tray, holes about
    6.5cm in diameter and 2cm deep,
    10 lightly greased or lined with
    10 paper muffin cases or 15cm
    baking parchment squares

Preheat the oven to 200°C/Gas mark 6. Sift the first five ingredients into a medium mixing bowl. Make sure they are evenly blended together by either mixing with a spoon or beating with an electric mixer for about 30 seconds on the lowest speed.

Next put the measured milk, yoghurt, egg, oil, chopped garlic leaves and three-quarters of the cheese into a large mixing jug or bowl. Beat together until well combined and the mixture is like a very thick batter. Pour into the dry ingredients and stir very lightly, scraping down the sides, until *just* combined, with no clumps of dry flour lurking in the bottom of the bowl.

Divide the mixture between the muffin cups, filling each to three-quarters full (this will be about one fully laden tablespoonful per cup). Place half a tomato, cut side uppermost, on the top of each muffin and sprinkle with the remaining cheese.

Bake in the oven for about 20 minutes until well risen and the tops are golden. The muffins should spring back into shape when lightly touched.

Savoury muffin variations

Follow the simple method of combining the dry ingredients, combining the wet ingredients, then mixing lightly together.

Cheese and Marmite This is my favourite! For the dry ingredients, use 250g plain flour, 2 tsp baking powder, ½ tsp bicarbonate of soda and 1 tsp English mustard powder. For the wet ingredients, use 125ml milk, 125ml plain yoghurt, 1 egg, 100ml sunflower oil, 125g grated mature Cheddar cheese and 2–3 tsp Marmite or other yeast extract. Finish with 5 cherry tomatoes, halved, and a sprinkling of grated cheese.

Blue cheese, apple and honey For the dry ingredients, use 250g spelt flour, 2 tsp baking powder and ½ tsp bicarbonate of soda. For the wet ingredients, use 125ml milk, 125ml plain yoghurt, 1 egg, 100ml rapeseed oil, 1 tbsp honey, 125g grated or finely crumbled blue cheese. Finish with 1 small apple, cored and finely sliced.

Anchovy and French dressing For the dry ingredients, use 250g plain flour, 2 tsp baking powder, ½ tsp bicarbonate of soda and 50g sunflower seeds. For the wet ingredients, use 125ml milk, 125ml plain yoghurt, 1 egg, 90ml French dressing and 2 tbsp anchovy essence. Finish with 5 cherry tomatoes, halved.

Blackberry and apple muffins

The beloved pairing of autumn blackberries and juicy apples makes the homeliest of muffins. Blackberries, those cherished gifts of the hedgerow, can be picked in season and frozen to use later in the year. For this recipe, you can use the blackberries straight from the freezer, but you will need to bake the muffins for 3–4 minutes longer.

Makes 10 large muffins

125g plain flour
125g wholemeal flour
2 tsp baking powder
½ tsp bicarbonate of soda
Pinch of sea salt
125ml milk
125ml plain yoghurt
1 egg
125g honey
100ml unsalted butter, melted and
    cooled
1 tsp vanilla extract

100–125g blackberries
1 medium dessert apple (100–125g),
    unpeeled, cored and finely diced
1 tbsp icing sugar, to finish

Equipment
12-hole muffin tray, holes about
    6.5cm in diameter and 2cm deep,
    10 lightly greased or lined with
    10 paper muffin cases or 15cm
    baking parchment squares

Preheat the oven to 200°C/Gas mark 6. Sift the first five ingredients into a medium mixing bowl. Make sure they are evenly blended together by either mixing with a spoon or beating with an electric mixer for about 30 seconds on the lowest speed.

Next put the measured milk, yoghurt, egg, honey, butter and vanilla extract into a mixing jug or bowl. Beat together until well combined and the mixture is like a very thick batter. Pour into the dry ingredients and stir very lightly, scraping down the sides, until *just* combined, with no clumps of dry flour lurking in the bottom of the bowl. Add the blackberries and diced apples and mix through lightly.

Divide the mixture between the muffin cups, filling each to three-quarters full (this will be about one fully laden tablespoonful per cup). For lightly crisp, glazed tops, dust with sifted icing sugar before they go into the oven. (Alternatively, dust with icing sugar once baked.)

Bake in the oven for about 20 minutes until well risen and the tops are golden. The muffins should spring back into shape when lightly touched.

Sweet muffin variations

Follow the simple method of combining the dry ingredients, combining the wet ingredients, then mixing lightly together.

Fruity fresh Replace the blackberries with blueberries, raspberries, strawberries or black- or redcurrants. Replace the apple with a dessert pear.

Mincemeat For the dry ingredients, use 125g plain flour, 125g wholemeal flour, 2 tsp baking powder, ½ tsp bicarbonate of soda, pinch of sea salt, 1 tsp ground cinnamon and 100g soft brown sugar. For the wet ingredients, use 125ml milk, 125ml yoghurt, 1 egg, 100ml sunflower oil and 4 tbsp mincemeat. To finish, use ½ red-skinned dessert apple, finely sliced, or 1 tbsp flaked almonds, plus 1 tbsp soft brown sugar.

Poppy seed For the dry ingredients, use 125g plain flour, 125g wholemeal flour, 2 tsp baking powder, ½ tsp bicarbonate of soda, pinch of sea salt, 125g caster sugar and 50g poppy seeds. For the wet ingredients, use 250ml buttermilk, 1 egg, 100ml rapeseed oil and the finely grated zest of an unwaxed lemon. While still hot from the oven, drizzle with the juice of 1 lemon mixed with 50g caster sugar.

Gooseberry friands

These moist, light-as-air little cakes are a breeze to make. I love this fragrant, zesty orange and gooseberry combination, but you could use any fresh fruit you like – raspberries, strawberries, a string of redcurrants, it really doesn't matter. What does matter is the burst of mouthwatering fruitiness when you bite into them. They're traditionally baked in special oval tins, but a deep muffin tray will do just as well.

Makes 12

175g unsalted butter
225g icing sugar
100g plain flour
125g ground almonds
6 egg whites
12 large gooseberries (red dessert
    or green)

To finish
Finely pared zest of 1 unwaxed orange
2 tbsp fresh orange juice
100g caster sugar

Equipment
12-hole friand or muffin tray, well
    greased and lightly dusted
    with flour

Preheat the oven to 200°C/Gas mark 6. Melt the butter in a pan over a low heat and set aside to cool slightly. Sift the icing sugar and flour into a mixing bowl, add the ground almonds and mix together thoroughly, then make a well in the middle.

Place the egg whites in a clean bowl and lightly whisk with a fork for 20–30 seconds, until they are just broken and combined. Pour into the well, with the melted butter. Stir lightly, but don't overdo it; the mixture should be gooey, soft and elastic.

Spoon the mixture into the prepared tins, filling each cup three-quarters full. Lightly place a gooseberry in the centre of each. Bake in the oven for 20–25 minutes or until the friands are pale golden and springy to the touch.

Meanwhile, put the orange zest in a small pan with a little water to cover. Bring to a simmer and cook for 10 minutes to soften, then drain and leave to dry.

When you take the friands from the oven, leave them in their tins for a few minutes. To remove from the tins, slide a knife down one side and the cakes should pop out – crisp, clean and irresistible. Transfer to a rack to cool.

Make a frosting by mixing the orange juice and caster sugar together. Leave for 15 minutes to allow the sugar to partially dissolve. Drizzle the frosting over the cooled cakes and top with a pinch of orange zest. Eat on the day you make them.

My chocolate brownies

Not that I like to crow, but over the years, my brownies have built up something of a reputation. You could almost say they are my trademark. So what's the secret? It's difficult to pinpoint but there are three things I consider important. Firstly, the eggs and sugar need to be whisked vigorously so the mixture increases vastly in volume. Secondly, I use a good-quality chocolate with 60–70% cocoa solids. Thirdly, and perhaps most importantly, these brownies must be made with love. Until now this recipe has been a closely guarded family secret, so please value it and use with reverence! These brownies are a celebration of pure indulgence...

Makes 12–16, depending on size

185g plain chocolate (60–70% cocoa
    solids), broken into small pieces
185g unsalted butter
1 tsp instant coffee (optional)
3 large eggs
275g golden caster sugar
85g plain flour
40g cocoa powder

50g white chocolate, roughly chopped
50g milk chocolate, roughly chopped

Equipment
25 x 20cm shallow baking tin, lightly
    greased and base-lined with
    baking parchment

Preheat the oven to 180°C/Gas mark 4. Put the plain chocolate in a heatproof bowl with the butter and coffee, if using. Place over a pan of barely simmering water or a very low heat and leave until melted. Stir to blend together and take off the heat.

Meanwhile, whisk the eggs and sugar together, using either a free-standing mixer or a hand-held electric whisk, until thick, pale and quadrupled in volume. This will take 4–5 minutes in a free-standing mixer, 8–10 minutes with a hand-held whisk.

Fold the chocolate mixture into the mousse-like egg mixture. Sift in the flour and cocoa powder, then, using a large metal spoon, fold in very carefully so as not to lose the tiny air bubbles. Finally, fold in the chopped white and milk chocolate.

Pour the mixture into the prepared tin and bake in the oven for about 35 minutes until the brownie no longer wobbles when softly shaken and the top is dark and shiny. Leave to cool in the tin.

When cold, carefully turn out onto a clean folded tea-towel to preserve the shiny top, then invert onto a board and cut into squares or triangles. These brownies can be stored for 4–5 days in an airtight tin, or for up to a week in a sealed container in the fridge.

Meringues

There is something rather magical about meringues, with their crisp shells and light-as-air middles. They team up perfectly with fresh fruit and/or ice cream and are gorgeous sandwiched together with a blob of clotted cream.

They require only a couple of ingredients and are fairly easy to make, though there are a few 'meringue secrets' to keep in mind. Success depends on incorporating oodles of air into the egg whites. Any trace of grease will thwart the eggs' ability to whisk to maximum volume, so you must use a spotlessly clean, dry bowl (best to avoid using a plastic one). The eggs should be at room temperature and, ideally, several days old. The sugar needs to be fine-grained to ensure it will dissolve quickly. Caster sugar is the norm, but icing sugar, soft brown sugar or a combination can be used to produce melt-in-the-mouth meringues.

Makes 10–12

3 egg whites
150g caster sugar, sifted icing sugar or soft brown sugar

Equipment
2 large baking sheets, lined with baking parchment

For near white, crisp, dry meringues Preheat the oven to 110°C/Gas mark ¼. Put the egg whites into a large mixing bowl and whisk, using a hand-held electric whisk until cotton wool-like and forming a stiff peak on the end of the whisk; do not over whisk or the whites will become dry and break down. Next, add the sugar, 1 tbsp a a time, whisking on medium speed until the mixture is stiff, with a glossy sheen.

Place tablespoonfuls of the mixture on the prepared baking sheet. Bake in the oven for 2–2½ hours or until the meringues are crisp and dry and come away easily from the baking sheet. Transfer to a wire rack to cool. When cold, store in an airtight container – they will keep for several weeks.

For light-golden, gooey-centred meringues Preheat the oven to 150°C/ Gas mark 2. Put the egg whites into a large mixing bowl and whisk, using a hand-held electric whisk, until the eggs are cotton wool-like and form a stiff peak on the end of the whisk; be careful not to over-whisk. Next, add the sugar, 1 tbsp at a time, whisking on a medium speed until the mixture is stiff, with a glossy sheen.

Place tablespoonfuls on the prepared baking sheet. Bake for about 40 minutes, or until the meringues are slightly golden and come away easily from the baking sheet. Remove to a wire rack to cool. Once cold, store in an airtight container – they will keep for several weeks.

Variation

Coffee meringues Use soft brown sugar and whisk 2–3 tsp coffee essence or instant coffee powder into the meringue mix after all the sugar has been added. Top each mound with a walnut half before putting into the oven.

Pip's hazelnut macaroons

My elder daughter Pip is a real whiz at making macaroons, so I turned to her to discover the secret of these chewy, nutty sweet treats. The chocolate-studded recipe that she's come up with is a real winner. Pip favours ground hazelnuts over the customary almonds. They are not as commonly available as ground almonds, but you can easily prepare them yourself: lightly toast the hazelnuts, then remove their skins (see p.32) before blitzing the nuts in a food processor until finely ground.

Cooked on baking parchment, these macaroons release very easily. However, Pip is still charmed by the fun of eating paper, so always bakes hers on rice paper.

Makes 10 (or 24 petits fours)
125g ground hazelnuts
150g caster sugar
2 egg whites
1 tsp vanilla extract
50g plain chocolate, chopped roughly
    into 1cm pieces

Equipment
**Large baking sheet lined with
    2 or 3 sheets of rice paper or
    baking parchment**

To finish
Whole hazelnuts

Preheat the oven to 180°C/Gas mark 4. In a medium mixing bowl, combine the ground hazelnuts and caster sugar.

In a separate bowl, lightly whisk the egg whites until white and frothy, but not stiff. Using a large metal spoon, lightly fold the egg whites into the nut and sugar mixture. When evenly combined, fold in the vanilla extract and chocolate pieces.

Place dessertspoonfuls of the mixture on the prepared baking sheet, leaving sufficient room in between for the macaroons to spread. (For petits fours macaroons, use a teaspoon instead.) Place a whole hazelnut in the centre of each biscuit.

Bake in the oven for 10–15 minutes until just firm and lightly coloured. Leave to cool on the baking sheet, then strip off the rice paper surrounding each one or simply use a palette knife to remove from the baking parchment.

Stored in an airtight tin, these macaroons will keep for 3–4 weeks.

Salt caramel shortbread

Gloriously self-indulgent and rather addictive, this lovely salty-sweet treat will wake up dull or sluggish taste buds. The sprinkle of sea salt brings out the creamy richness of the sweet caramel, while at the same time complementing the pure, smooth dark chocolate. Make sure you use a soft, sweet-tasting, unrefined natural salt – Maldon, Halen Môn or Cornish sea salt – and good-quality chocolate.

Makes 12

For the shortbread base
150g unsalted butter, softened
75g caster sugar
150g plain flour
75g semolina

For the caramel layer
½ tsp flaky sea salt
1 quantity Caramel cream (see p.51)

For the chocolate topping
150g plain chocolate, chopped
25g butter
1 tsp flaky sea salt

Equipment
20cm square, 5cm deep baking tin,
    lightly greased and base-lined with
    baking parchment

Preheat the oven to 170°C/Gas mark 3. Put the butter in a bowl and gradually work in the sugar, using a wooden spoon, until well mixed to a soft paste. Sift in the flour and semolina. Using a fork, bring together to form a soft, crumbly dough. Knead as lightly as possible, until you have a soft, pliable, crack-free dough. (Or put the butter, sugar, flour and semolina into an electric mixer and mix on low speed until the mix starts to come together, then increase the speed a little to knead lightly.)

Press this shortbread dough into the baking tin and lightly prick the surface with a fork. Bake in the oven for 30 minutes or until lightly coloured and firm to the touch. Leave in the tin until completely cool.

For the caramel layer, sprinkle the salt into the caramel cream and mix until well blended, then smooth over the shortbread base. Refrigerate for 30 minutes.

In the meantime, put the chocolate into a heatproof bowl with the butter and place over a pan of barely simmering water (making sure the bowl isn't touching the water) until just melted. Remove from the heat.

Pour the melted chocolate over the caramel-topped shortbread and immediately sprinkle with the 1 tsp sea salt. Leave (if you can) for at least a couple of hours to firm up. Cut as required into squares, fingers or sweet canapé bites. These shortbreads will keep for up to 2 weeks in an airtight tin.

Florentines

Florentines, bedecked and bejewelled with glacé fruit and nuts, are redolent of luxury and riches, and very high-ranking in the biscuit hierarchy. However, despite their overt flamboyancy, they are quick, easy and very satisfying to make. Appealing and rather special, half a dozen will delight any beneficiary lucky enough to receive them.

Makes 12

75g unsalted butter
75g light soft brown sugar
25g (about 1 tbsp) honey (runny or thick)
1 tbsp plain yoghurt
50g finely chopped preserved stem ginger (drained of its syrup)
100g dried pears, sliced into long strands
50g glacé cherries, quartered

50g hazelnuts, toasted and roughly chopped (see p.32)
40g plain flour – white, spelt or chestnut flour
125g chocolate – plain, milk or white, broken into small pieces

Equipment
2 large baking sheets, lined with baking parchment

Preheat the oven to 180°C/Gas mark 4. Put the butter, brown sugar and honey into a heavy-based saucepan. Heat very gently over a low heat, stirring, until the butter has melted and the mixture is absolutely smooth. Remove from the heat.

Stir the yoghurt into the mixture, then add the ginger, pears, glacé cherries and hazelnuts; mix well. Finally, sift in the flour and fold in with a large metal spoon.

Place generous dessertspoonfuls of the mixture onto the prepared baking sheets, spacing them about 5cm apart to allow room for a little spreading (like middle age). With the back of a spoon or fork, flatten each to a 5cm round.

Bake in the oven for about 20 minutes until lightly browned and slightly crisp around the edges, or allow a little longer if you prefer a very crisp biscuit.

Leave the Florentines on the baking sheet for 10–15 minutes to firm up. When cool and firm enough to handle, use a palette knife (or your fingers) to release them, flip them over and transfer to a wire rack to cool completely.

Put the chocolate into a heatproof bowl and place over a pan of hot water, making sure the basin isn't actually touching the water. Leave until the chocolate has just melted and is smooth and glossy.

Now you need to coat the smooth bottoms of the Florentines with the melted chocolate. The easiest way to do this is to spoon the chocolate onto the centre of the Florentine base, then spread it evenly with a flat-sided knife that has been dipped into a jug of very hot water.

Leave to set, chocolate side uppermost, on a wire rack. The Florentines will keep for up to 10 days stored in an airtight tin.

Variations
Replace the stem ginger with mixed candied peel, the pears with dried apricots, and/or the hazelnuts with flaked almonds.

Big Cakes

Bring back teatime

and tablecloths! This chapter features the darlings of the old-fashioned teatime cake trolley: Madeira cake, coffee cake, cherry cake, the indomitable Victoria sandwich. Their familiar and comforting names, unchanged for generations, are like badges of honour, signifying their faithful service as the great classics of the tea table.

Many of these great cakes share the same origin. They are descendants of the 'pound cake', a traditional recipe using equal weights of the four main ingredients – butter, sugar, flour and eggs – sometimes delicately flavoured with a hint of citrus or finished with a filling of jam. But this simple foundation can be embellished with more indulgent ingredients, such as cocoa, coffee, fruit or nuts, to create delectable wholesome cakes. These uncomplicated – somehow rather pure – cakes serve as a splendid base for rich icings and creamy fillings; they can also be infused with fresh-tasting or aromatic drizzles and syrups.

While the cakes in this chapter are particularly well suited to a proper sit-down high tea, the less rich examples will agreeably fit the bill at different times of the day. A chunk of homely Apple cake (see p.138) is totally justifiable mid-morning, for instance, while a little nibble of lightly spiced Cardamom cake (see p.159) is welcome whenever friends drop by.

There are also cakes here that lead double lives, by which I mean those that are overtly confident and adept at fitting into more than one occasion. Equally at home on the tea table or as the last course of a meal, these are what I call 'pudding cakes'. Frequently enriched with a little fresh fruit and yoghurt or cultured cream, they are neither too sweet nor too rich and therefore great to eat at any time of the day – or night for that matter.

I hope you will get great pleasure from baking the cakes in this chapter. Be adventurous and be prepared to improvise as well. If, for example, you find you only have two eggs when the recipe says three, improvise and make up the difference with a splash of milk. And, of course, you can adapt the flavourings or alter the finish of the cake as the fancy takes you.

Victoria sandwich

If you only ever make one cake, let it be the glorious Victoria sandwich. The simple mix of equal quantities of eggs, butter, sugar and flour, sandwiched together with raspberry jam, is unquestionably the queen of British cakes. It has long reigned supreme at the tea table, the village fête and the garden party – indeed, a freshly baked Victoria sandwich will lend itself to almost any occasion.

Originally, to make a perfect cake, the eggs were first weighed in their shells and the exact equivalent weights of butter, sugar and flour were measured out. With the strict grading of eggs these days, it's not essential to do this, but I would stick to this rule if you're not sure precisely what size your eggs are – for instance, if you keep hens yourself. If you are buying eggs in a shop, I recommend using medium ones to equal the quantities of the other ingredients in this recipe.

Get to know this recipe if you can, not least because it forms the basis of all manner of other cakes. With the addition of a few well-chosen extra ingredients, the classic Victoria can swiftly be altered to almost any flavour you fancy (see variations overleaf). You can also use this recipe to make cup cakes.

Serves 8–10

175g self-raising flour
Pinch of sea salt
175g unsalted butter, cut into small
  pieces and softened
175g caster or vanilla sugar, plus
  extra to finish
3 medium eggs, lightly beaten
1 tsp vanilla extract
3–4 tbsp soft-set raspberry jam

Equipment
2 x 20cm sandwich tins or a 23cm
  round tin, lightly greased and
  base-lined with baking parchment

NOTE For total egg weight less than
  175g use 2 x 18cm sandwich tins,
  or a 20cm round tin

Preheat the oven to 180°C/Gas mark 4. Sift the flour and salt together into a bowl and put aside.

In a large mixing bowl, using either a wooden spoon or a hand-held electric whisk, beat the butter to a cream.

Add the caster sugar and continue to beat until the mixture is very light and creamy (this will take about 5 minutes with a hand-held electric whisk and up to 10 minutes using a wooden spoon). The lighter and fluffier the butter and sugar mix is, the easier it will be to blend in the eggs, which in turn helps to prevent the mixture curdling (see p.42).

(continued overleaf)

Add the eggs, about a quarter at a time, adding 1 tbsp of the weighed-out flour with each addition and beating thoroughly before adding the next. Beat in the vanilla extract with the last of the egg.

Sift in the rest of the flour, half at a time, and use a large metal spoon to carefully fold it in. The mixture should drop off the spoon easily when tapped against the side of the bowl. If it doesn't, then add a spoonful or two of hot water.

Divide the mixture equally between the prepared sandwich tins (or spoon it all into the larger cake tin if using), spreading it out lightly and evenly with the back of a spoon. Bake in the centre of the oven for about 25 minutes or until the cake(s) are lightly golden and spring back into shape when gently pressed with a finger.

Leave the cake(s) in the tin(s) for a couple of minutes before turning them out onto a wire rack to cool completely. (If you've baked a single cake, once cooled, cut it horizontally into two equal layers.)

When cold, spread one cake layer with the jam, place the second on top and dust lightly with caster sugar. The cake will keep for 5 days in an airtight tin.

Variations

Fillings and toppings Instead of raspberry jam, fill with any other favourite jam or homemade Lemon curd (see p.50), or fill and top with chocolate hazelnut spread. Instead of sprinkling with sugar, top with Glacé icing (see p.55). Or, in the summer, fill with strawberries or raspberries and whipped cream and dust with icing sugar.

Heavenly scented Place 3 or 4 deliciously scented geranium leaves, such as Mabel Grey or Attar of Roses, in the base of the lined tin. Remove when the cake is turned out to cool.

Chocolate Replace 25g of the flour with cocoa powder. Fill the cake with Chocolate buttercream (see p.49) and top with Chocolate glacé icing (see p.55), or fill and top with Chocolate crème fraîche topping (see p.65).

Coffee Omit the vanilla. Dissolve 1 tbsp instant coffee in 1 tbsp hot water and add to the mixture with the final egg. Fill and top with Coffee buttercream (see p.49).

Victoria cup cakes Bake the mixture in one or two well-greased or paper-lined muffin trays; there should be enough to make 18 cup cakes. When cool, split in half and fill with jam and whipped cream.

Genoese sponge

The texture of a classic Genoese sponge – light yet pleasantly firm – lends itself to many uses. It's lovely cut into layers and sandwiched together with Buttercream (see p.49) and soft-set jam; or topped with whipped cream and a pile of fresh berries; or lightly drizzled with a fruit or liqueur syrup, dusted with icing sugar and served with a fresh fruit compote. It's also perfect for a traditional trifle.

Serves 12–14

125g plain flour
Pinch of sea salt
4 eggs
125g caster sugar
75g unsalted butter, melted and
   cooled

Equipment
23cm round or 20cm square tin,
   or 2 x 20cm deep sandwich tins,
   sides lightly greased and lightly
   dusted with flour, and base-lined
   with baking parchment

Preheat the oven to 180°C/Gas mark 4. Sift together the flour and salt twice and set aside. Have ready a large saucepan half full of simmering water, over which a heatproof mixing bowl will fit without touching the water.

Put the eggs and sugar in the heatproof bowl and place over the pan of simmering water. Using a hand-held electric whisk, beat at top speed for about 8 minutes until the mixture has at least tripled in size, is very pale and thick – it should hold a 'ribbon' on the surface when the whisk is lifted. Remove the bowl from the heat. (Or use a free-standing electric mixer; it will take about 5 minutes at its highest speed.)

Sift half the sifted flour over the mixture and use a large metal spoon to carefully fold it in. Repeat with the remaining flour. Dribble the melted butter over the surface a little at a time and then carefully but quickly fold it into the mixture, to minimise the loss of volume.

Pour the mixture into the prepared tin(s) and bake in the oven for 25–30 minutes, or until the cake is golden brown, firm and springs back into shape when lightly pressed. If you are using sandwich tins, the baking time will be barely 25 minutes. Leave in the tin(s) for 10 minutes before turning out onto a wire rack to cool.

When cold, the cake(s) will keep for a couple of days in an airtight tin, or they can be frozen for up to 6 weeks. Once filled, a Genoese sponge is best eaten on the day.

Variation
Chocolate Genoese Replace 25g of the flour with cocoa powder.

Zesty lemon Madeira cake

The name of this lovely light, buttery cake derives from the Victorian habit of enjoying a glass of Madeira alongside it. It's a shame we no longer do the same (though feel free). A classic English recipe, using classic cake ingredients, you'll find its homely aroma will fill the kitchen and beyond in the most pleasing way.

I like to top my Madeira cake with a zesty lemony icing. However, you can serve it un-iced, in which case I think it's nice to scatter some strips of candied citron peel (available from health food stores) over the cake before baking.

Serves 10

For the cake
200g plain flour
1 tsp baking powder
150g unsalted butter, cut into
    small pieces and softened
Finely grated zest of 2 unwaxed
    lemons, plus 2 tbsp juice
150g golden granulated sugar
4 eggs

For the topping
150g icing sugar
1½ tbsp lemon juice
Fresh, crystallised or sugared violets,
    or candied citron peel

Equipment
1 litre loaf tin, about 20 x 10cm lightly
    greased, base and long sides lined
    with baking parchment

Preheat the oven to 180°C/Gas mark 4. Sift the flour and baking powder together and set aside.

In a mixing bowl, beat the butter with the lemon zest, using either a wooden spoon or a hand-held electric whisk, to a cream. Add the sugar and continue to beat until the mixture is very light and creamy. Add the eggs one at a time, adding 1 tbsp of the flour with each and beating thoroughly before adding the next egg. Fold in the remaining flour, using a large metal spoon, then fold in the 2 tbsp lemon juice.

Spoon the mixture into the prepared tin and spread out lightly and evenly with the back of the spoon. Bake in the oven for about 50 minutes until the cake is well risen, springy to the touch and a skewer inserted in the centre comes out clean. Leave in the tin for 10 minutes before turning out onto a wire rack to cool.

Meanwhile, for the topping, sift the icing sugar into a bowl. Beat in the lemon juice, a little at a time, until the icing is glossy and fairly stiff. Spread thickly on top of the cake and decorate with violets or candied citron peel.

This cake will keep for 10 days in an airtight tin.

Coffee and walnut cake

This traditional cake never fails to please; its bitter-sweet flavours make it one of my all-time favourites. I like to use old-fashioned Camp coffee essence for the coffee bit. Still made in Scotland, this iconic dark brown syrup is a blend of chicory and coffee. It dates back to 1876 when it was used by the military as an easy-to-prepare hot drink for sustaining troops during foreign campaigns. However, you can use instant coffee or very strong freshly brewed coffee instead.

Serves 10

For the cake
200g plain flour
1½ tsp baking powder
200g unsalted butter, cut into small
    pieces and softened
100g light soft brown sugar
100g caster sugar
3 eggs
50ml coffee essence (or 1 tbsp instant
    coffee dissolved in 1 tbsp boiling
    water, or 3 tbsp very strong
    fresh coffee)
100g chopped walnuts
25–50ml milk

For the buttercream
60g unsalted butter, cut into small
    pieces and softened
125g icing sugar, sifted
10ml coffee essence (or 2 tsp instant
    coffee dissolved in 2 tsp boiling
    water or 1 tbsp strong fresh coffee)

For the topping
200g icing sugar
2 tsp coffee essence (or 2 tsp instant
    coffee dissolved in 2 tbsp boiling
    water, or 1 tbsp strong fresh coffee)
50g chopped walnuts

Equipment
2 x 20cm sandwich tins, lightly
    greased and base-lined with
    baking parchment

Preheat the oven to 180°C/Gas mark 4. Sift the flour and baking powder together and set aside.

In a large mixing bowl, using either a wooden spoon or a hand-held electric whisk, beat the butter to a cream. Add the brown and caster sugars and beat until light and creamy. Add the eggs, one at a time, adding 1 tbsp flour with each and beating thoroughly before adding the next. Stir in the coffee essence.

Now carefully fold in the remaining flour, half at a time, with a large metal spoon. Fold in the chopped walnuts and sufficient milk to give a soft dropping consistency.

Spoon the mixture into the prepared tins, spreading it out evenly with the back of the spoon. Bake in the oven for 25–30 minutes until the tops are a light golden brown and the cakes spring back into shape when gently pressed. Leave in the tins for 10 minutes before turning out to cool on a wire rack.

Meanwhile, prepare the buttercream. Beat the butter to a cream, add the icing sugar and the coffee essence and beat until light and creamy.

To make the glacé icing for the topping, sift the icing sugar into a bowl, add the coffee essence and 1–2 tbsp boiling water, and mix until thick.

Spread one of the cooled cakes with the buttercream. Sandwich together with the second cake and cover the top with glacé icing. Finish with the chopped walnuts. This cake will keep for a week in an airtight tin.

Variation

Streusel-topped coffee cake Spoon the cake mixture into one 23cm round tin. To make the streusel topping, mix together 125g light soft brown sugar, 50g plain flour, 1 tsp ground cinnamon, 125g chopped walnuts and 50g melted butter until evenly combined. Sprinkle over the surface of the cake mixture in the tin and bake for 40–45 minutes until golden brown on top.

Chocolate cake

Of all cakes, this is the one with the highest expectations, but fear not, I promise this recipe will meet the toughest standards. For the perfect dreamy chocolate experience, I recommend filling and topping the cake with my fudgy icing, but you might like to verge into Black Forest territory with the white choc-cherry variation. Either way, the cake is at its best a day or two after making, when cake and filling have subtly and deliciously become one.

Serves 12–16

For the cake
25g cocoa powder
25g drinking chocolate powder
200g plain flour
1 tsp baking powder
1 tsp bicarbonate of soda
Good pinch of sea salt
175g unsalted butter, cut into small
   pieces and softened
100g light soft brown sugar
100g caster sugar
4 eggs
150ml buttermilk (or 75ml whole
   milk mixed with 75ml plain yoghurt)
100g ground almonds

For the filling and topping
2 x quantity Chocolate fudge icing
   (see p.63)
50g plain chocolate, finely grated

Equipment
23cm round loose-bottomed cake tin
   or 2 x 20cm sandwich tins, 5cm
   deep, sides well greased and
   base-lined with baking parchment

Preheat the oven to 180°C/Gas mark 4. Put the cocoa powder and drinking chocolate into a small bowl. Add 50ml freshly boiled water, mix to a paste and set aside. Sift the flour, baking powder, bicarbonate of soda and salt together and set aside.

In a large mixing bowl, using either a wooden spoon or a hand-held electric whisk, beat the butter to a cream. Add both the sugars and the cocoa paste. Continue beating until light and very creamy. Add the eggs one at a time, adding 1 tbsp of the flour with each and beating thoroughly before adding the next. Then fold in the remaining flour with the buttermilk little by little – dry, wet, dry, wet – until you have a very soft, creamy mixture. Finally, carefully fold in the ground almonds.

Spoon the mixture into the prepared tin(s), spreading it out lightly and evenly with the back of the spoon. Bake in the oven, allowing 45–50 minutes for a cake in a 23cm tin and 35–40 minutes for cakes in 20cm deep sandwich tins.

Leave the cake(s) in the tin(s) for 10 minutes before turning out and placing on a wire rack to cool completely.

When cold, cut the 23cm cake into three layers, or each of the 20cm cakes into two layers. Sandwich the layers together with the chocolate fudge icing, saving sufficient to smother over the top. Finish the top with a sprinkling of grated chocolate. This cake will keep for 5–6 days in an airtight tin.

Variations

Black Forest Combine 200g warm cherry or damson jam with 200g melted white chocolate. Use to layer the cake together and top with Chocolate icing (see p.63) and Chocolate leaves (see p.65).

Triple-layer cake Halve the listed quantities and bake the cake in an 18cm round tin. Assemble as above.

Wholemeal orange cake
with Earl Grey icing

The bergamot orange is one of those slightly confused citrus fruits that doesn't quite know what it is. Its flavour lies somewhere between a sweet orange and a grapefruit, but it is yellow in colour and could be mistaken for a lemon, were it not for its slightly pear-like shape. Unquestionably, it is the bergamot's fragrant oil, used to flavour and scent Earl Grey tea, which gives this muddled fruit its status in the citrus world. The combination of a surprisingly light wholemeal orange cake and an aromatic Earl Grey icing is a firm favourite with my family.

Serves 8–10

For the cake
100g self-raising wholemeal flour
75g self-raising white flour
1 tsp baking powder
Pinch of sea salt
175g unsalted butter, cut into small
  pieces and softened
Finely grated zest of 1 unwaxed
  orange, plus the juice of
  ½ orange (50ml)
175g caster sugar
3 eggs

For the filling
1 quantity Cream cheese topping
  flavoured with orange zest
  (see p.57)

For the topping
1 Earl Grey tea bag
250g unrefined icing sugar
12 walnut halves

Equipment
2 x 20cm sandwich tins, lightly
  greased and base-lined with
  baking parchment

Preheat the oven to 180°C/Gas mark 4. Sift the wholemeal and self-raising flours together with the baking powder and salt; set aside.

In a large mixing bowl, beat the butter and orange zest to a cream, using either a wooden spoon or a hand-held electric whisk. Add the sugar and continue to beat until the mixture is very light and fluffy. Beat in the eggs one at a time, adding 1 tbsp flour with each. Using a large metal spoon, fold in the remaining flour. Finally fold in the orange juice.

Spoon the mixture into the prepared tins, spreading it out lightly and evenly with the back of the spoon. Bake in the oven for about 25 minutes until cooked and the centre springs back into shape when lightly touched with a finger.

Leave the cakes in the tins for 5–10 minutes before turning out and placing on a wire rack to cool. When cold, sandwich together with the cream cheese filling.

For the Earl Grey icing, infuse the tea bag in 2 tbsp boiling water for about 5 minutes, then remove. Sift the icing sugar into a bowl. Little by little, add the tea to the icing sugar, beating until thick and glossy. Using a palette knife, spread the icing evenly over the top of the cake. Decorate with the walnut halves.

This cake will keep for 3–4 days in an airtight tin.

Apple cake

You should be able to throw this homely country cake together easily, since it uses ingredients that we usually have in our kitchens. You can make it with cooking or dessert apples, whichever is to hand. To peel or not to peel? For new season's apples, I'd say leave the skins on, but older or waxy-skinned ones are best peeled.

Serves 10

For the cake
125g self-raising white flour
125g self-raising wholemeal flour
½ tsp bicarbonate of soda
2 tsp ground nutmeg
½ tsp ground cloves
Pinch of sea salt
125g unsalted butter, cut into
    small pieces
125g soft brown sugar
350g cored apples (prepared weight)
1 egg, beaten
50ml milk

For the topping
1 small eating apple (ideally red-
    skinned, cored but not peeled
1 tbsp caster sugar

Equipment
23cm round loose-bottomed or
    springform tin, or a 20cm square
    loose-bottomed tin, greased and
    base-lined with baking parchment

Preheat the oven to 180°C/Gas mark 4. Sift the first six ingredients into a large bowl and mix well together. Add the butter and, using your fingertips, rub it into the flour until the mixture resembles medium breadcrumbs. Stir in the sugar. Cut the apples into 1cm dice and toss lightly in the rubbed-in mixture until evenly distributed. Add the egg and milk and bring the mix together with a wooden spoon to a sticky, lumpy dough. Spoon into the prepared tin and level with the back of the spoon.

For the topping, cut the apple across into 7 or 8 slices and poke out any residual pips embedded in the flesh. Lay the apple slices on top of the cake. Sprinkle the caster sugar evenly over the mixture and apples (to give the cake a lovely crisp topping).

Bake for 45–50 minutes until the top is golden brown, firm and crispy to the touch. Leave in the tin for 20–30 minutes before turning out onto a wire rack. This cake will keep for 2–3 days in an airtight tin in a cool place.

Variation

Special day apple cake Soak 125g sultanas in a little brandy and add to the mix with the chopped apple. Sprinkle 2 tbsp flaked almonds over the top before baking.

Carrot cake

High in natural sugars and full of juice, carrots have long been valued as ingredients in cakes and puddings. Carrot cake is also known as 'Passion cake', because it was once made as a cheaper alternative to a formal richly fruited wedding cake. All that love and fervour – no wonder carrot cake is such a perpetual favourite.

Serves 8–10

For the cake
125g self-raising wholemeal flour
1 tsp ground mixed spice
1 tsp baking powder
Pinch of sea salt
150g unsalted butter, cut into small
    pieces and softened
Finely grated zest of 1 orange
150g golden caster sugar
3 eggs
75g ground almonds
250g finely grated carrot
75g sultanas or raisins
75g flaked almonds or chopped walnuts

For the topping
1 quantity Cream cheese topping
    (see p.57)
75g Marzipan, shaped into carrots
    (see p.59), to decorate (optional)

Equipment
20cm round or 18cm square tin,
    lightly greased and base-lined with
    baking parchment

Preheat the oven to 180°C/Gas mark 4. Sift together the flour, mixed spice, baking powder and salt into a bowl and set aside.

In a large mixing bowl, beat the butter and orange zest to a cream, using either a wooden spoon or a hand-held electric whisk. Add the sugar and continue to beat until the mixture is light and fluffy.

Add the eggs, one at a time, adding 1 tbsp of the flour mix with each and beating thoroughly before adding the next. Using a large metal spoon, fold in the remaining flour mix, followed by the ground almonds, grated carrot, dried fruit and nuts.

Spoon the mixture into the prepared tin, smoothing it out gently with the back of the spoon. Bake in the oven for 45–50 minutes until the cake is evenly coloured and springs back into shape when lightly pressed with a finger. Leave in the tin for 10 minutes before turning out onto a wire rack to cool.

When the cake is cold, spread with the cream cheese topping. Finish with marzipan carrots, if using. This cake will keep for 3–4 days in an airtight tin in a cool place.

Old-fashioned cherry cake

The glacé cherry plays a supporting role in lots of recipes. It lends glamour to fruit cakes, crystal-like jewels to Florentines and very often it's the cherry on top of the cake! Allow it sovereignty and you will truly appreciate its flavour and texture. Undoubtedly one of my favourites, cherry cake is an absolute teatime classic.

Serves 10

For the cake
250g natural undyed glacé cherries
75g plain flour, plus ½ tbsp to dust
    cherries
100g self-raising flour
Pinch of sea salt
175g unsalted butter, cut into small
    pieces and softened
175g caster sugar
3 eggs
100g ground almonds
2 tsp vanilla extract
75ml milk, to mix

To finish
Glacé icing (see p.55)
3–4 glacé cherries, halved
3–4 pieces candied angelica (optional)

Equipment
2 litre loaf tin, about 25 x 13cm,
    lightly greased and lined with
    baking parchment, or a 20cm
    round or 18cm square tin
    lightly greased and base-lined
    with baking parchment

Preheat the oven to 180°C/Gas mark 4. Start by rinsing the sticky sugar syrup off the cherries. To do this, place them in a sieve and rinse with a little warm water. Dry thoroughly with a piece of kitchen paper, then cut the cherries in half and toss with ½ tbsp plain flour; set aside. Sift the flours and salt together.

In a large mixing bowl, using either a wooden spoon or hand-held electric whisk, beat the butter to a cream. Add the sugar and continue beating until the mixture is very light and fluffy. Add the eggs, one at a time, adding 1 tbsp of the flour with each and beating thoroughly before adding the next egg.

Fold in the remaining flour, ground almonds and the glacé cherries. Add the vanilla extract and incorporate sufficient milk to give a light dropping consistency.

Spoon the mixture into the prepared tin, smoothing over the surface with the back of the spoon. Bake in the oven for 55–60 minutes until evenly cooked and the centre springs back when lightly touched with a finger.

Leave the cake to cool in the tin for 10 minutes before turning out and placing on a wire rack to cool completely.

To finish, spread the glacé icing evenly over the surface of the cake. Decorate with glacé cherry halves and finely cut strips of angelica. This cake will keep for about a week in an airtight tin.

Variations

Cherry and chocolate Instead of glacé icing, top with bitter-sweet Chocolate crème fraîche topping (see p.65) and decorate as above.

Fresh cherry For a summertime special, use fresh rather than glacé cherries. Rinse the cherries, dry well and remove the stones before adding to the mixture.

Marble cake

The fun of the marble cake is that no piece is ever the same – each slice is a work of art in itself, which is why it has fascinated children for generations. The success of the marbling depends on how the uncooked mixture is spooned into the tin. Keep the spoonfuls irregular in size and not too big and hopefully your cake will be swirly and patterned throughout. Alternatively, this easy recipe can be baked unmarbled – either all chocolate or all vanilla – to make a lovely plain cake or to use as a base for other flavours or fruity drizzles.

Serves 10

300g self-raising flour
200g unsalted butter, cut into small
    pieces and softened
250g caster sugar
3 eggs
200ml soured cream
25g cocoa powder
2 tsp vanilla extract

Equipment
20cm round or 18cm square tin,
    lightly greased and base-lined
    with baking parchment

Preheat the oven to 180°C/Gas mark 4. Sift the flour into a bowl and set aside.

In a mixing bowl, using either a wooden spoon or a hand-held electric whisk, beat the butter to a cream. Add the sugar and continue to beat until the mixture is very light and creamy. Add the eggs, one at a time, adding 1 tbsp of the flour with each and beating thoroughly before adding the next. Beat in the soured cream until evenly combined. Using a large metal spoon, carefully fold in the remaining flour.

Divide the mixture between two bowls. Into one, sift the cocoa powder and carefully fold in. To the second, add the vanilla extract and gently blend in.

Without being too neat and tidy, drop dessertspoonfuls of each mixture alternately into the prepared tin. When they are all added, tap the tin sharply on the work top to level the surface, then lightly swirl a skewer through the mixture to give the cake its distinctive marbled look.

Bake in the oven for 45–50 minutes until the cake is evenly golden and springs back into shape when lightly pressed.

Leave in the tin for 10 minutes before turning out to cool on a wire rack. This cake will keep for up to a week in an airtight tin.

Gill's honey cake

This well-loved recipe comes from Gill Meller, head chef at River Cottage, and it is frequently served to guests at Park Farm. One of the lovely things about this cake is that the taste will vary depending on the honey you choose. Try, if you can, to use a local honey. Not only will this be uniquely flavoured by the flowers and blossoms of your region, it's better for the environment too – bee miles, unlike other air miles, don't count towards your carbon footprint!

Serves 10

300g unsalted butter, cut into
    small pieces and softened
250g caster sugar
4 eggs
150g self-raising wholemeal flour
1 tsp baking powder
150g ground almonds
50g flaked almonds
4 tbsp runny honey (or set honey,
    warmed sufficiently to trickle)

Equipment
23cm springform cake tin, or
    a 20cm square loose-bottomed
    tin, lightly greased and base-lined
    with baking parchment

Preheat the oven to 170°C/Gas mark 3. In a large mixing bowl, beat the butter to a cream. Add the sugar and beat thoroughly until very light and fluffy. Beat in the eggs, one at a time, adding a spoonful of the flour with each and beating thoroughly before adding the next.

Combine the remaining flour with the baking powder and sift into the bowl. Using a large metal spoon, carefully fold into the mixture. Stir in the ground almonds until evenly mixed.

Spoon the mixture into the prepared tin, spreading it evenly with the back of the spoon. Scatter over the flaked almonds. Stand the tin on a baking sheet (as the cake may leak a little butter during cooking). Bake in the oven for about 45 minutes, until springy to the touch and a skewer inserted into the centre comes out clean.

On removing from the oven, trickle the honey over the surface so that it soaks into the hot cake. Leave in the tin for half an hour or so before turning out and placing on a wire rack to cool completely.

This cake is best kept for a day or two before eating. It keeps well for at least a week, stored in an airtight tin.

Golden syrup cake

I'm not going to try and convince you that this is a 'healthy' cake, but it certainly is irresistible. Amber in colour with a sweet, honey-like flavour, the golden syrup gives it a unique and delicious savour, while breadcrumbs lend a lovely light texture. Fantastic with mid-morning coffee or packed in a lunch box, it also makes an easy pud – served warm with custard or ice cream.

Serves 8–10

250g golden syrup
100g unsalted butter, cut into cubes
150g self-raising flour
½ tsp bicarbonate of soda
½ tsp fine sea salt
50g fresh white breadcrumbs
Finely grated zest of ½ unwaxed lemon
1 egg
150ml plain yoghurt

Equipment
1 litre loaf tin, about 22 x 10cm,
    lightly greased, base and sides
    lined with baking parchment

Preheat the oven to 180°C/Gas mark 4. Put 200g of the golden syrup and the butter in a small saucepan, place over a low heat and stir until the butter has melted and combined with the syrup. Set aside to cool.

Meanwhile sift the flour, bicarbonate of soda and salt into a medium mixing bowl. Add the breadcrumbs and lemon zest and mix together until well combined. Make a well in the centre.

In another bowl, lightly beat the egg and mix in the yoghurt. Pour into the well in the dry ingredients and add the cooled syrup mixture. Using either a wooden spoon or a hand-held electric whisk on medium speed, beat until smooth and glossy.

Pour the mixture into the prepared tin and bake in the oven for about 40 minutes until the surface is evenly golden and the cake springs back when lightly touched. Shortly before the cake will be ready, mix the remaining golden syrup with 1 tbsp freshly boiled water.

As you take the cake from the oven, prick the surface deeply (but not right through to the bottom) all over with a skewer. Pour the warm syrup evenly over the surface. Leave the cake in the tin until cool before turning out.

This cake will keep for 5–6 days in an airtight tin.

'Men only' lemon drizzle

The village horticultural show throws up no end of emotions on show day: angst, resentment, joy, disbelief and elation, to name a few. A win turns you giddy with success, whereas a harsh comment from a judge can hurt and humiliate. There's always fierce competition in the 'Men only' class – daggers drawn and all that stuff. Rob Prosser kindly gave me the recipe for his winning lemon drizzle cake.

Serves 8

For the cake
175g self-raising flour, sifted
1 tsp baking powder
175g caster sugar
175g unsalted butter, cut into
    small pieces and softened
Finely grated zest of 2 unwaxed
    lemons
3 eggs

For the drizzle
Juice of 2 lemons
100g granulated sugar

Equipment
18cm round or 15cm square tin,
    greased and base-lined with baking
    parchment, or a 1 litre loaf tin,
    approx 20 x 10cm, greased, base and
    long sides lined with parchment

Preheat the oven to 180°C/Gas mark 4. Sift the flour and baking powder into a mixing bowl. Add all the other cake ingredients and, using a hand-held electric mixer, beat for about 1½ minutes, until you have a smooth, thick batter. Spoon the mixture into the prepared tin, levelling out the surface with the back of a spoon.

Bake for 40–45 minutes or until the surface is golden brown and a skewer inserted into the centre of the cake comes out clean. Leave in the tin for about 10 minutes before turning out and placing on a wire rack.

Meanwhile, prepare the drizzle. Mix the lemon juice with the granulated sugar; do not let the sugar dissolve. Prick the surface of the warm cake all over with a skewer and carefully trickle the drizzle over the surface, a spoonful at a time, ensuring each addition has soaked in before spooning over the next. Leave to cool completely.

This cake will keep for 5 days in an airtight tin.

Variation

Mincemeat cake Spoon half the cake mixture into the prepared tin, spread 3–4 tbsp mincemeat over the surface and top with the remaining cake mix. Sprinkle with 1–2 tbsp flaked almonds and bake as above. Omit the lemon drizzle.

Lime and coconut cake
(gluten free)

Creamy coconut and zesty lime team up perfectly to flavour this lovely gluten-free cake. Because the recipe uses rice flour rather than conventional wheat flour, it does have a tendency to sink a bit in the middle. This doesn't bother me in the least – in fact, I rather enjoy the dense centre. However, if you're concerned about it, you can prevent the cake sinking by adding a little xanthan gum, which acts as a substitute for the stretchy, bouncy gluten found in wheat flours and will bind the mixture together. Xanthan gum is available from health food stores and the baking section of larger supermarkets.

Serves 10–12

For the cake
125g rice flour
2 tsp gluten-free baking powder
1 tsp xanthan gum (optional)
175g unsalted butter, cut into
    small pieces and softened
Finely grated zest of 3–4 small limes
175g caster sugar
3 eggs
50g desiccated coconut

For the drizzle
75g caster sugar
100ml freshly squeezed lime juice
    (about 3–4 limes)

Equipment
1 litre loaf tin, approx 20 x 10cm,
    lightly greased, base and long sides
    lined with baking parchment, or
    a 20cm round or 18cm square tin,
    lightly greased and base-lined with
    baking parchment

Preheat the oven to 180°C/Gas mark 4. Sift together the rice flour, baking powder and xanthan gum, if using, into a bowl.

In a mixing bowl, beat the butter and lime zest to a cream, using either a wooden spoon or a hand-held electric whisk. Add the sugar and continue to beat until the mixture is light and creamy. Add the eggs, one at a time, adding 1 tbsp flour with each and beating thoroughly before adding the next. Carefully fold in the remaining flour with a large metal spoon, then fold in the desiccated coconut.

Spoon the mixture into the prepared tin, lightly smoothing over the surface with the back of a spoon. Bake in the oven for 40–45 minutes or until the surface is nicely golden and the cake feels springy to the touch. Shortly before the cake will be ready, prepare the drizzle by dissolving the sugar in the lime juice.

When the cake comes out of the oven, prick the surface deeply (but not to the very bottom) all over with a skewer. Spoon half the lime syrup over the surface and leave to cool for 10 minutes before spooning over the remainder. Make sure you pour plenty of drizzle down the sides of the tin. Leave in the tin until cool before turning out.

This cake will keep for 5 days in an airtight tin.

Variations

St Clement's cake Replace the limes with a mix of lemons and oranges.

Christmas cracker Replace the limes with tangerines. For the drizzle, replace 50ml of the juice with 50ml orange liqueur.

Bounty bar cake

Inspired by a well-known chocolate bar, this dense, chocolatey wonder is an adaptation of my mother's recipe for a moist coconut cake. The coconut needs to soak for a couple of hours, so remember to start well before you're planning to bake the cake.

Serves 10

For the cake
50g desiccated coconut
150ml full-fat or reduced-fat coconut milk (or you can use ordinary milk)
150g self-raising flour
25g cocoa powder
150g caster sugar
150g unsalted butter, cut into small pieces and softened
2 eggs

To finish
1 quantity Chocolate crème fraîche topping (see p.65)
Large chocolate buttons, to decorate

Equipment
1 litre loaf tin, approx 20 x 10cm, lightly greased, base and long sides lined with baking parchment, or a 20cm round tin, lightly greased

Preheat the oven to 180°C/Gas mark 4. Put the desiccated coconut into a bowl and pour on the coconut milk (or ordinary milk). Leave for a couple of hours to swell and rehydrate.

Sift the flour and cocoa powder into a mixing bowl. Add the sugar and mix until evenly distributed, then add the butter and eggs. Using a hand-held electric whisk, beat for about 1½ minutes until the mixture is light and creamy. Carefully stir in the coconut, along with any residual liquid, mixing until well combined.

Spoon the mixture into the prepared tin, levelling the surface with the back of the spoon. Bake in the centre of the oven, allowing about 40 minutes for a cake in a loaf tin, 25–30 minutes for a round cake. When done, the cake should spring back into shape when lightly pressed.

Leave to cool in the tin for 10 minutes before turning out and placing on a wire rack. Leave to cool completely.

To finish, spread the chocolate crème fraîche topping evenly over the top of the cake and decorate with chocolate buttons.

This cake will keep for 5 days in an airtight tin.

Caraway and orange cake

The joy of this cake is that you need only one bowl and one measure. Using a 150ml yoghurt pot (or any other 150ml measure), you'll be able to knock it up effortlessly wherever you are. You can leave it plain, or flavour it as you choose. I love to add caraway – to make a sweetly aromatic, old-fashioned seed cake – but I realise not everyone shares my passion for this feisty little seed. If you're not so keen, try one of my suggested variations (below).

Serves 8–10

1 tbsp caraway seeds
2 x 150ml pots plain full-fat or
    semi-skimmed yoghurt
½ x 150ml pot (75ml) rapeseed oil
2 eggs
2 x 150ml pots caster sugar
Finely grated zest of 1 unwaxed orange
3 x 150ml pots plain flour
¼ x 150ml pot flaked almonds

Equipment
2 litre loaf tin, about 25 x 13cm, or
    a 1 litre loaf tin, approx 20 x 10cm,
    for a deeper cake, lightly greased,
    base and long sides lined with
    baking parchment

Preheat the oven to 180°C/Gas mark 4. Heat a small frying pan over a medium heat for a couple of minutes, then add the caraway seeds and toast them gently for 2–3 minutes, stirring constantly, until they become fragrant. Pound the seeds lightly (they don't have to be reduced to a powder) to release their sweet, aromatic flavour.

Put the yoghurt, oil, eggs, sugar and orange zest into a large mixing bowl and beat with a wooden spoon to a smooth, creamy batter. Sift in the flour and beat lightly until well incorporated. Spoon into the prepared tin and sharply tap the tin on the work surface to level the mixture. Sprinkle the flaked almonds evenly over the top.

Bake in the oven for 45–50 minutes until golden brown and a skewer inserted in the centre of the cake comes out clean. Leave in the tin for 20 minutes or so before removing to a wire rack to cool. This cake will keep for a week in an airtight tin.

Variations

Plain Jane Omit the caraway seeds and flaked almonds.

Poppy seed and lemon Replace the caraway with poppy seeds and the orange with lemon zest. Mix the juice of 1 lemon with 100g granulated sugar and pour over the hot baked cake – the juice will sink in and the sugar will form a crunchy topping.

Swiss roll with poppy seeds
and lemon curd filling

The Americans call this type of cake a 'jelly roll', while the French know it as *gâteau roulé*. No one is quite sure why we call this feather-light, rolled-up sponge a Swiss roll. It doesn't seem to have any particular link with Switzerland. In fact, this simple rolled cake – or something like it – is made the world over. You can easily alter the recipe by adding flavourings to the sponge or by tinkering with the all-important gluey filling. In this case, some delightfully sharp lemon curd sets off the sweet, nutty flavour of the poppy seeds in the sponge.

Serves 8

For the cake
75g plain flour
Pinch of sea salt
3 eggs
75g caster sugar
2 tbsp poppy seeds

For the filling
1 quantity Lemon curd (see p.50)

To finish
Caster sugar, for dusting
Icing sugar, for dusting (optional)

Equipment
20x35cm Swiss roll tin, base-lined
with baking parchment, and sides
and base lightly greased and
dusted with flour

Preheat the oven to 190°C/Gas mark 5. Sift the flour and salt together into a bowl and set aside.

Place the eggs and sugar in a large mixing bowl. Using either a hand-held electric whisk or a free-standing electric mixer, whisk until the mixture has almost quadrupled in volume, is very light and fluffy, and holds its shape. This will take around 7–8 minutes with a hand-held whisk and 4–5 minutes in a free-standing electric mixer.

Add 1 tbsp warm water and fold in carefully. Sift half of the flour over the mixture and sprinkle in 1 tbsp of the poppy seeds. Using a large metal spoon, carefully fold them in before adding the remaining flour and poppy seeds in the same way. Scrape down the sides of the bowl well with a spatula.

Pour the mixture into the prepared tin and spread it out lightly and evenly, making sure it fills the corners of the tin.

Bake in the oven for 12–14 minutes until the sponge feels firm to the touch in the centre.

Have ready a piece of greaseproof paper 10cm larger all round than the Swiss roll tin. Lay the paper on your work surface and dust lightly with caster sugar.

As soon as the sponge comes out of the oven, turn it onto the sugared paper. Remove the tin and carefully peel away the baking parchment. Roll up the cake from the short side, rolling the sugared paper inside the cake as you go. Lift onto a wire rack and leave to cool.

When you are ready to fill the sponge, carefully unroll it. Spread the lemon curd over the sponge, leaving a 1cm margin free all around. Then, using the greaseproof paper as a guide, re-roll the cake. Place it, seam side down, on a wire rack or serving plate and dust with caster or icing sugar before serving.

This will keep for 3 days in an airtight tin but it is best eaten within a day or two.

Variations

Traditional Swiss roll Omit the poppy seeds. Add 1 tsp vanilla extract instead with the egg and sugar. Replace the lemon curd filling with your favourite jam.

Chocolate Swiss roll Replace 25g of the flour with cocoa powder. Blend 100ml plain yoghurt with 100g chocolate hazelnut spread and use for the filling.

Cardamom cake

I love the smell of this cake: the mellow, warming fragrance of cardamom lingers enticingly long after the cake has been taken from the oven. And I love the fact that it's so simple to make: no vigorous beating or whisking and only one bowl to wash up. But most of all I love this cake because it's just so very good. Enjoy it with good coffee or even a glass of sweet Sauternes and you'll see what I mean.

It is a flat cake and sometimes it can sink a bit – but don't worry, just think of this as another of its charms. Incidentally, it's a useful recipe if you are catering for someone who can't eat eggs. Note that you need the lemony seeds from green cardamom pods, not the camphor-flavoured seeds of the black cardamom.

Serves 8–10

About 20 green cardamom pods
250g self-raising flour
Pinch of sea salt
½ tsp bicarbonate of soda
100g unsalted butter, cut into
    small pieces
200g caster sugar
300ml crème fraîche

To finish
Caster sugar or icing sugar,
    for dredging

Equipment
20cm round tin, greased and
    base-lined with baking
    parchment

Preheat the oven to 170°C/Gas mark 3. Split the green cardamom pods open, remove the seeds and grind with a pestle and mortar or spice grinder. Sift the flour, salt, bicarbonate of soda and ground seeds together into a bowl and set aside.

Warm the butter gently in a small pan until it has just melted; do not allow it to get too hot. Put the sugar in a large bowl. Add the butter and beat for a minute or so. Add the crème fraîche and beat until you have a thick creamy batter.

Incorporate the flour mix, a third at a time, folding it in carefully with a large metal spoon. The mixture will be quite sticky and dough-like. Spoon into the prepared tin, spreading it out evenly and gently with the back of the spoon.

Bake in the oven for 50–60 minutes until the top is golden brown and the cake springs back into shape when lightly touched. Allow to cool for 5–10 minutes before turning out onto a wire rack, bottom side up, to cool.

Now you have the choice of either dredging the top with caster sugar while the cake is hot or leaving it until it is cold and dusting liberally with icing sugar. This cake will keep for 5 days in an airtight tin.

Scent from heaven cake
(lemon verbena)

My garden is crowded with herbs and in early summer, when they are abundant and most fragrant, I instil their uplifting essence into my baking whenever I can. Often these self-effacing plants shy away from attention by producing insignificant flowers. But crush their shapely leaves and they release the most exquisite of perfumes. A few sprigs of an intensely aromatic herb can absolutely transform an otherwise simple cake. Lightly infuse the herb in water and the resulting liquor can be added to drizzles, icings and – in the case of this recipe – the cake itself.

Serves 10–12

For the cake
5–6 lemon verbena sprigs
100g plain flour
1 tsp baking powder
200g ground rice
200g unsalted butter, cut into
    small pieces and softened
150g caster sugar
3 eggs

To finish
100g icing sugar, sifted
4–5 lemon verbena leaves

Equipment
2 litre loaf tin, about 25 x 13cm, or
    an 18cm square tin, sides lightly
    greased and base-lined with
    baking parchment

Preheat the oven to 180°C/Gas mark 4. Strip the lemon verbena leaves off the stalks. Place 5 or 6 leaves on the lined base of the tin. Put the rest into a measuring jug and cover with 200ml freshly boiled water, making sure all the leaves are completely immersed to prevent them oxidising and discolouring. Set aside to cool.

Sift the flour and baking powder into a bowl, add the ground rice and mix well to combine; set aside.

In a large mixing bowl, using either a wooden spoon or a hand-held electric whisk, beat the butter to a cream. Add the sugar and beat until light and creamy. Incorporate the eggs one at a time, adding a spoonful of the flour mix with each one, and beating thoroughly before adding the next. Using a large metal spoon, carefully fold in the remaining flour mix.

Strain the verbena-infused water. Add 100ml to the cake mixture, reserving the rest, and gently fold it in, to give a very soft dropping consistency. Spoon the mixture into the prepared tin, smoothing it evenly and lightly with the back of the spoon.

Bake in the oven for about 50 minutes until the cake is lightly golden and springs back into shape when gently pressed. Just before it is done, prepare the drizzle by mixing the remaining 100ml verbena-infused water with the icing sugar and stirring until dissolved.

As the cake comes out of the oven, prick it all over deeply (but not to the bottom) with a skewer and spoon half the drizzle over the surface. Leave for 10 minutes, then spoon over the remainder, making sure you pour plenty down the sides of the tin.

Leave the cake in the tin until cool before turning out. Arrange the lemon verbena leaves on top to decorate. The cake will keep for 5 days in an airtight tin.

Variations

Rose-scented geranium Replace the lemon verbena with a few leaves of a scented geranium such as Mabel Grey or Attar of Roses.

Lavender with lemon Replace the lemon verbena with either 2 tbsp fresh lavender flowers or 1 tbsp dried ones. Prepare the drizzle by dissolving 100ml caster sugar in 100ml lemon juice.

Chocolate and peppermint Replace the lemon verbena with fresh peppermint leaves and 25g of the flour with cocoa powder.

'Hebegebe' cake
(courgette and chocolate)

Hebe, the naughtiest dog we've ever had, is a retriever by name, but not by nature. Find a cake she certainly can, but retrieve it she will not. Instead, she'll scoff the lot. That is what she did the first time I made this lovely moist courgette cake. I took it as a resounding vote of confidence in the recipe and named the cake in Hebe's honour. Incidentally, this is a great way to use up some of those overgrown courgettes that seem to swell to monster proportions in the garden overnight.

Serves 12

175g unsalted butter, cut into
    small pieces and softened
175g golden granulated sugar
3 eggs, beaten
100ml plain yoghurt
1 tsp vanilla extract
250g plain flour, sifted
1½ tsp baking powder
3 tbsp cocoa powder
About 250g courgettes, unpeeled,
    finely grated
150g chocolate (plain, milk, white or a
    mix), roughly cut into 1.5cm chunks

Equipment
20cm square or 23cm round tin,
    lightly greased and base-lined with
    baking parchment

Preheat the oven to 180°C/Gas mark 4. In a mixing bowl, beat the butter to a cream. Add the sugar and, using either a wooden spoon or a hand-held electric whisk, beat until light and creamy. Gradually add the eggs, one at a time, beating well after each addition. Mix in the yoghurt and vanilla extract.

Combine the flour, baking powder and cocoa powder. Sift them into the mixture, one third at a time, using a large metal spoon to carefully fold them in. Stir in the grated courgettes and half of the chocolate. Pour into the prepared tin and sprinkle the remaining chocolate pieces over the top.

Bake for 45–50 minutes until the cake is firm but springy to the touch. Leave in the tin (out of dog reach) for 20 minutes before turning out and placing on a wire rack to finish cooling. This cake will keep for 3 days stored in an airtight tin. For longer keeping, store in the fridge.

Banana and chocolate cake

Black, blighted and limp they may be, but don't throw those overripe bananas away. This is a great recipe for using them up. In fact, really ripe fruits lend much more flavour to a cake than under-ripe ones. I pop overlooked bananas into the freezer until I have sufficient to make a cake. They go even blacker and I do get the odd sideways glance from anyone who comes across them. However, any dubious comments are withdrawn when a freshly baked banana cake is up for grabs.

Serves 10–12

225g self-raising flour
½ tsp bicarbonate of soda
125g unsalted butter, cut into
    small pieces and softened
125g soft brown sugar
2 large eggs
2–3 very ripe bananas
    (250–300g when peeled)
150ml plain yoghurt
2 tsp vanilla extract
100g plain or milk chocolate, roughly
    cut into 1.5cm chunks

Equipment
23cm garland or ring mould,
    well greased, or a 20cm round cake
    tin, lightly greased and base-lined
    with baking parchment

Preheat the oven to 180°C/Gas mark 4. Sift together the flour and the bicarbonate of soda into a bowl. Set aside.

In a large mixing bowl, beat the butter and sugar together, using a wooden spoon or a hand-held electric whisk, until the mixture is light and creamy. Beat in the eggs, one at a time, adding 1 tbsp of the flour with each.

Mash the bananas to a thick purée and beat into the mixture. Stir in the yoghurt and vanilla extract. Using a large metal spoon, fold in the remaining flour, followed by the chocolate pieces.

Spoon the mixture into the prepared tin, spreading it evenly with the back of the spoon. If using a ring mould, tap it firmly on the work surface to level the mixture. Bake in the oven for about 30 minutes, until the cake is well risen and will spring back into shape when lightly touched.

Leave in the tin for 5 minutes before turning out onto a wire rack to cool completely. Once cold, this cake will keep for 3–4 days in an airtight tin.

Seville orange polenta cake (gluten free)

The first of the Seville oranges arrive from Spain in January. Too bitter and acidic to be eaten raw, these citrus fruits are full of flavour and quintessential for marmalade-making. Their distinctive taste is also excellent in cakes, such as this lovely gluten-free cake, which is deliciously lightly spiced with warming cloves. When it's closed season for Sevilles, you can ring the citrus changes by using lemons, limes or sweet oranges instead.

Serves 12

For the cake
125g fine polenta
225g ground almonds
1 tsp baking powder
½ tsp ground cloves
225g unsalted butter, cut into
    small pieces and softened
200g caster sugar
Finely grated zest of 3 Seville oranges
3 eggs

For the drizzle
100ml Seville orange juice
    (2–3 oranges)
50g golden caster sugar
3 or 4 cloves

Equipment
23cm loose-bottomed or springform
    cake tin, well greased and base-lined
    with baking parchment

Preheat the oven to 170°C/Gas mark 3. Put the polenta, ground almonds, baking powder and ground cloves into a bowl and mix together well.

In another mixing bowl, beat the butter to a cream, using either a wooden spoon or a hand-held electric whisk. Add the sugar and half the orange zest and continue to beat until light and fluffy. Incorporate the eggs one at a time, beating well before adding the next. Using a large metal spoon, carefully fold in the polenta and almond mix. Spoon into the prepared tin, spreading evenly with the back of the spoon.

Bake in the oven for about 50 minutes until golden on top and springy to the touch. Shortly before the cake is done, prepare the orange drizzle by gently warming the orange juice, remaining orange zest, the sugar and whole cloves in a small pan until the sugar has dissolved, then simmer for a couple of minutes.

While the cake is still hot, prick the surface with a skewer or cocktail stick and spoon the orange syrup carefully over it. Leave to cool in the tin before turning out. Once cold, this cake will keep for 5–6 days in an airtight tin.

Somerset cider cake
with hazelnut topping

This moist yet light-textured cake, with its crumbly nutty topping, will be subtly different depending on the type of cider you use. With more than 400 different apple varieties growing throughout the West Country's ciderlands, there's plenty of choice, from 'Slack my Girdle' to 'Tremlett's Bitter'. A sweet cider will blush the cake pink, while a bitter-sharp brew will lend a lightly golden hue. A couple I like to use here are the fruity Somerset Redstreak and the aromatic Kingston Black.

Serves 10–12

For the cake
150g raisins
250ml sparkling cider
125g plain flour
125g plain wholemeal flour
Pinch of sea salt
1 tsp bicarbonate of soda
½ whole nutmeg, freshly grated
125g unsalted butter, cut into
    small pieces and softened
125g light soft brown sugar
3 eggs

For the topping
50g unsalted butter, cut into
    small pieces
75g soft light brown sugar
25g plain flour
½ tsp freshly grated nutmeg
75g hazelnuts, chopped

Equipment
20cm springform cake tin, lightly
    greased and base-lined with
    baking parchment

Preheat the oven to 180°C/Gas mark 4. Place the raisins in a small bowl and pour over 100ml of the cider. Leave in a warm place to plump up for a couple of hours or overnight, if you have time.

To make the nutty topping, put the butter into a small pan and warm over a gentle heat until it has just melted. Remove from the heat and add the rest of the topping ingredients. Lightly mix together until well combined. Set aside.

For the cake, sift the flours, salt and bicarbonate of soda together into a bowl. Add the grated nutmeg and set aside.

In a mixing bowl, beat the butter to a cream, using either a wooden spoon or a hand-held electric whisk. Add the sugar and continue to beat until the mixture is soft and creamy. Add the eggs, one at a time, adding 1 tbsp of the sifted flour with each and beating thoroughly before adding the next.

Sift in half of the remaining flour and use a large metal spoon to carefully fold it in. Add the rest of the cider to the mix and gently stir in (it will foam up enthusiastically). Sift in the remaining flour and lightly fold it in. Finally, incorporate the cider-soaked raisins, together with any liquor.

Spoon the mixture into the prepared tin, spreading it out evenly with the back of the spoon. Sprinkle the topping over the surface.

Bake in the oven for 45–50 minutes, until the cake is golden brown and a skewer inserted in the centre comes out clean. Leave in the tin for 30 minutes before turning out and transferring to a wire rack to cool completely.

The cake will keep for a week stored in an airtight tin.

Variations

Soak the raisins in cider brandy rather than cider. Use walnuts instead of hazelnuts.

Raspberry Battenberg cake

The Battenberg, sometimes called the 'church window cake', is such a pretty thing to create. Although it may look difficult, it's easy and fun to make and quite heavenly to eat. It's simply a cake of two flavours, stuck together with raspberry jam and wrapped up in soft, sweet almond marzipan. Using fresh raspberries to colour the pink bit means an escape from bottled food colouring, and also gives a fabulous fresh fruit flavour.

Once you've mastered this raspberry and vanilla combination, you'll dream up lots of other scrummy alternatives. You could even add a third flavour – chocolate works well – building a cake of six squares.

Serves 12

For the cake
100g raspberries (either fresh or
    frozen and defrosted)
175g caster sugar, plus 1 tsp for
    the raspberries
100g rice flour
1½ tsp baking powder
100g ground almonds
175g unsalted butter, cut into
    small pieces and softened
3 eggs
¼ tsp vanilla paste or ½ tsp
    vanilla extract

To finish
150g soft-set raspberry jam
Icing sugar, for dusting
450g Marzipan (see p.58)

Equipment
2 x 1 litre loaf tins, approx 20 x 10cm,
    lined with baking parchment

Preheat the oven to 180°C/Gas mark 4. Start by making the pink colouring for the cake. Place the raspberries in a small bowl and mix in 1 tsp caster sugar. Leave until the juices begin to run, then use the back of a spoon to crush the fruit to a pulp. Sieve to remove the pips. Set aside.

Sift the rice flour and baking powder into a mixing bowl and mix thoroughly. Add the ground almonds, butter, sugar and eggs. Using either a wooden spoon or a hand-held electric whisk, beat for a couple of minutes until all the ingredients are well combined and the mixture is light and creamy.

Divide the mixture in half and place in two bowls. Add 2 tbsp of the raspberry purée to one portion and the vanilla to the other. Carefully mix the flavouring into each portion until well blended.

(continued overleaf)

Spoon the raspberry mixture into one prepared loaf tin and the vanilla mixture into the other, smoothing them both evenly and lightly with the back of the spoon. Bake in the oven for 25–30 minutes until evenly coloured and firm to the touch. Leave the cakes in their tins for 5–10 minutes before removing and transferring to a wire rack to cool completely.

When cool, carefully trim off the ends of each cake, then slice each one lengthways in two, so you have four rectangles, exactly the same size. Brush the strips of cake with raspberry jam and sandwich them together, alternating the raspberry and vanilla strips, to create the characteristic chequered pattern.

Next dust your work surface with icing sugar and roll out the marzipan to a rectangle, about 20x32cm (or big enough to wrap around your cake). Brush the top of the cake with raspberry jam and invert the cake onto the centre of the marzipan. Brush the remaining three sides with raspberry jam. With jam-free fingers, wrap the marzipan round the remaining three sides of the cake and press the edges together to make a neat join. Carefully invert the cake, so the seam is underneath.

To finish, use your finger and thumb to crimp and decorate the top edges, then very lightly score the top of the cake with a knife to create a criss-cross pattern.

This cake will keep for a week stored in an airtight tin.

Variation

Chocolate and hazelnut Battenberg Replace the almonds with ground hazelnuts. Instead of using raspberries to colour one half of the cake pink, replace 25g of the rice flour with 25g cocoa powder. Use chocolate hazelnut spread to bond the cake pieces together, rather than raspberry jam.

Hugh's fresh cherry cake
with streusel topping

Available for only a few weeks of the year, delicious homegrown cherries are highly seasonal. What's more, these summer gems are as coveted by the blackbirds as they are by us. Anyone lucky enough to have a cropping cherry tree will have to pit themselves against these feathered foragers in order to gather in a harvest. Otherwise you'll need to keep a sharp eye out for them in farm shops, markets or your local greengrocer's. Bringing home even a small bag of these lovely cherries is worthwhile, though, as this gorgeous pudding cake from Hugh F-W shows. The crumbly, nutty streusel topping is a crunchy delight.

Serves 8

For the cake
- 125g unsalted butter, cut into small pieces and softened
- 125g caster sugar
- 2 eggs
- 75g self-raising white or wholemeal flour
- 75g ground almonds (ready-ground or whizzed in a food processor)
- 1 tsp almond extract (optional but lovely if you like that extra-almondy, frangipane taste)
- 300g fresh cherries, stoned and halved

For the topping
- 25g plain white or wholemeal flour
- 25g ground almonds
- 50g caster sugar
- 25g unsalted butter, cut into small pieces
- 50g blanched almonds, slivered (see p.32)

Equipment
20cm springform cake tin, lightly greased and base-lined with baking parchment

Preheat the oven to 180°C/Gas mark 4. Start by making the streusel topping. Sift the flour into a mixing bowl. Add the ground almonds and caster sugar and stir to combine. Rub in the butter, using your fingertips, until the mixture resembles coarse breadcrumbs. Set aside.

For the cake, in a mixing bowl, using either a wooden spoon or hand-held electric whisk, beat the butter to a cream. Add the caster sugar and continue to beat until the mixture is light and fluffy. Add the eggs one at a time, incorporating 1 tbsp of the flour with each, and beating until thoroughly combined before adding the next. Stir in the ground almonds and almond extract, if using. Sift in the remaining flour and fold in gently, using a large metal spoon.

Spoon the cake mixture into the prepared tin, smoothing it out evenly and gently with the back of the spoon. Lay the cherries over the top of the mixture. Sprinkle the streusel topping evenly over the cherries and then scatter the slivered almonds all over the top.

Bake in the oven for 45–50 minutes, until the almonds are lightly browned and a skewer inserted into the centre of the cake comes out clean. Leave for 10 minutes before releasing the tin and moving the cake to a wire rack to cool.

This cake is delicious warm or cold, with custard (if serving warm) or clotted cream or Greek yoghurt. It will keep for up to 3 days in an airtight tin.

Variations

Plum and walnut cake For the cake, replace the cherries with halved plums and the ground almonds with walnuts. For the topping, replace the ground almonds with porridge oats and the slivered almonds with chopped walnuts.

Apricot and almond cake For the cake, replace the cherries with halved apricots.

P.S. To help save the British cherry, visit www.foodloversbritain.com and look up their CherryAid campaign.

Toffee apple cake

Heavy with sweet apples and creamy caramel, this scrumptious cake is just the thing to use up the glut of orchard apples that a good cropping year provides.

Serves 8–10

For the cake
3–4 medium eating apples, such as Cox's or Russets
125g dark soft brown sugar
175g self-raising flour
1 tsp baking powder
½ tsp fine sea salt
175g golden caster sugar
175g unsalted butter, cut into small pieces and softened
3 eggs

For the filling
1 quantity Caramel cream (see p.51)

Equipment
2 x 20cm sandwich tins, lightly greased and base-lined with baking parchment

Preheat the oven to 180°C/Gas mark 4. Core, peel and quarter the apples. Slice each quarter into 4 or 5 thin slices. Place the brown sugar in a bowl, add the apple slices and toss until well covered. Starting from the outside and working inwards, arrange the apples over the base of each prepared tin, finishing with a ring in the centre.

Sift the flour, baking powder and salt into a large mixing bowl and mix thoroughly. Add the caster sugar, butter and eggs. Using either a wooden spoon or a hand-held electric whisk, beat together for a couple of minutes until the mixture is light, creamy and well blended.

Divide the mixture equally between the apple-lined tins, spreading it out evenly with the back of the spoon. Bake the cakes in the oven for about 25 minutes or until lightly golden and they spring back into shape when gently touched with a finger.

Leave the cakes in the tins for 10 minutes, before carefully turning out and placing on a wire rack. Remove the parchment to reveal the rich brown caramelised apples.

When completely cold, sandwich the two cakes together with a generous layer of caramel cream. This cake is best eaten within a couple of days.

Variation

Turn the apples in 3 or 4 tbsp of marmalade instead of the brown sugar. For the filling, use marmalade instead of caramel cream.

Plum upside-down cake

The plum season stretches from mid-July until October, starting with the small, blushing hedgerow cherry plums and ending with their dark-skinned cousins. This is a lovely recipe to use whatever variety comes your way. It can easily be adapted to use other stone fruits or blackberries, blueberries or gooseberries. I like to serve it slightly warm, with a dollop of fromage frais or clotted cream.

Serves 8–10

For the cake
200g self-raising flour
Pinch of sea salt
200ml buttermilk
2 tsp vanilla extract
100g unsalted butter, cut into
    small pieces and softened
125g caster sugar
2 eggs

For the upside-down top
About 500g plums (any variety)
100g runny honey (or set honey,
    slightly warmed)
2–3 tsp rose water

Equipment
23cm round loose-bottomed or
    springform cake tin, greased and
    base-lined with baking parchment

Preheat the oven to 180°C/Gas mark 4. First prepare the top of the cake. Halve the plums lengthways with a sharp knife. Twist them apart and remove the stone with the point of the knife. Use small cherry plums in halves, quarter larger Victoria-type plums or slice very large plums. Arrange the plums, cut side down, over the base of the tin. Trickle over the honey and sprinkle with the rose water. Set aside.

Sift the flour and salt together and set aside. Combine the buttermilk and vanilla extract in a jug; put to one side.

In a mixing bowl, beat the butter to a cream, using a wooden spoon or a hand-held electric whisk. Add the sugar and beat until light and creamy. Add the eggs, one at a time, adding 1 tbsp of the flour with each, and beating thoroughly before adding the next. Incorporate the remaining flour and the buttermilk little by little – dry, wet, dry, wet – until evenly combined and you have a soft dropping consistency.

Spoon the mixture over the plums, spreading it out evenly with the back of the spoon. Bake in the oven for 45–50 minutes until the cake is golden and the juices from the fruit are bubbling around the edge.

While the cake is still warm, place a flat plate on the tin and turn out. This cake is best eaten when freshly made but it will keep for a couple of days in a cool place.

Rhubarb pudding cake
with custard

Forced in warm, dark growing sheds (or under rhubarb bells), the tender blush-pink stalks of early rhubarb are our first homegrown crop of the year. This attractive pudding cake is a wonderful way to savour their fresh and exhilarating newness. Of course, later in the season, outdoor-grown, or 'field' rhubarb, can be used instead, but it is often a little more tart, and doesn't have the exquisite colour and tenderness of the early shoots. You can easily adapt this recipe using other homely comfort-pud combinations (see variations), any of which can be enjoyed as a pudding or as a teatime treat.

Serves 10

250g rhubarb (trimmed weight), sliced into 5mm pieces
200g self-raising flour, plus 1 tbsp for dusting
50g custard powder or cornflour
½ tsp bicarbonate of soda
125g unsalted butter, cut into small pieces and softened
175g golden caster sugar
3 eggs

150ml plain yoghurt
2 tsp vanilla extract
1 tbsp rose water (optional)
Custard or clotted cream, to serve

Equipment
23cm ring tin, well greased, or a 20cm loose-bottomed round tin, lightly greased and base-lined with greaseproof paper

Preheat the oven to 180°C/Gas mark 4. Put the rhubarb into a bowl, sprinkle with 1 scant tbsp self-raising flour and toss until the pieces are all covered. This floury coating will help to prevent the rhubarb sinking in the cake.

Sift the flour, custard powder or cornflour and bicarbonate of soda together into a bowl. Set aside.

In a large mixing bowl, using either a wooden spoon or a hand-held electric whisk, beat the butter to a cream. Add the sugar and beat together until very light and fluffy. Beat in the eggs, one at a time, adding 1 tbsp of the flour mix with each, and beating thoroughly before adding the next. Stir in the yoghurt, vanilla extract and rose water, if using. Fold in the remaining flour followed by the sliced rhubarb.

Spoon the mixture into the prepared tin, levelling the surface with the back of the spoon or giving the tin a good sharp tap on the work surface to level the mix.

Bake in the oven for 40–45 minutes until the cake is well risen and springs back into shape when lightly pressed. Leave in the tin for 10 minutes before turning out onto a wire rack to cool.

Serve the pudding cake either warm with custard, or cold just as it is or with a dollop of clotted cream. It keeps for a couple of days in an airtight tin. If you want to keep it for any longer, put it in the fridge.

Variations

Raspberry and rice cake Replace the rhubarb with raspberries and the custard powder with rice flour.

Blackberry and semolina cake Replace the rhubarb with blackberries and the custard powder with semolina.

Potato and apple cake

This traditional Irish recipe typifies how easy it is to take everyday ingredients and speedily turn them into something scrumptious. Peel a few extra spuds when making mash and you'll have enough for this cake. Of course you can glam it up a bit by adding a spoonful or two of rum-soaked raisins or a handful of hedgerow blackberries to the apples. Or for a savoury note, add a little grated Cheddar to the potato dough. However, I like it most of all made simply with the unassuming, but very worthy, cooking apple.

Serves 4–8 (depending on appetites)

For the cake
500g mashed potatoes
25g unsalted butter, melted
125g plain flour
1 tsp baking powder
1 tsp sea salt
400g cooking apples
Pinch of ground cloves

To finish
25g unsalted butter, cut into
 4 slices
100g caster sugar

Equipment
Large baking sheet, lightly floured

Preheat the oven to 200°C/Gas mark 6. Place the mashed potatoes in a mixing bowl (if using freshly cooked potatoes allow them to dry off first). Add the melted butter and sift in the flour, baking powder and salt. Using a wooden spoon or your hand, bring together to form a soft, smooth dough. Divide the mixture in two.

On a floured surface, shape each portion of dough into a 20cm circle, then place one round on the baking sheet. Peel, core and finely slice the apples. Layer them on top of the dough to within 1cm of the edge and dust with the ground cloves. Dampen the edge of the dough with a little water. Place the second dough round on top. Seal the edges by lightly turning with the sides of your hands, moulding until the cake is neatly formed with a flat top and is about 3cm deep. Using a sharp knife, lightly score a cross on the surface and make a small hole in the centre.

Bake in the oven for 35–50 minutes until golden. Remove from the oven and, working quickly from the centre, lightly prise back each quarter and insert the butter slices and sugar, then replace the dough. Return to the oven for 5 minutes to allow the butter to melt.

This cake is best by far when eaten fresh from the oven, but any left over will not disappoint when cold.

Fruity Cakes
& Gingerbread

The proud descendants of the great cakes of old feature in

this chapter, their ancestral roots stemming back to the sweet fancies of the medieval period. At that time, such treats were no more than a basic bread dough, enriched with added ingredients such as butter, honey, dried fruits and spices. The extra ingredients were scarce and costly, so bakers were banned from producing this type of confection for any occasion other than the festivities of the Christian calendar: Christmas, Easter, weddings, christenings and funerals.

Fruit cakes come from extensive families and include a good number of regional variations. Their outward appearance is understated, yet their insides are a sweet medley of aromatic and wholesome ingredients. More often than not, early fruit cakes were termed 'plum cakes', simply because of the inclusion of dried plums (prunes) in the recipes – a prudent and good use of the late-summer plum harvest. These days, the plums have been replaced by raisins, sultanas and currants in nearly all recipes. Favoured for their exceptional keeping quality, good fruit cakes are also delectably moreish.

Gingerbreads take their name from their sixteenth-century ancestors, which did in fact contain grated bread. These hard, flat gingerbreads – often made in the shape of men or numbers – were a combination of grated bread, ginger, aniseed, liquorice and pepper, sweetened with honey and mixed to a stiff paste with ale. In due course, flour, eggs and fat replaced the bread, and treacle took the place of the honey. Thick, moist gingerbreads, as we know them today, came about in the nineteenth century, when bicarbonate of soda was added to the list of ingredients, helping to leaven and lighten the dough.

Bastions of the cake tin, both gingerbreads and fruit cakes will, I hope, become firm favourites of your baking repertoire.

P.S. The expression 'baker's dozen' originates from the practice of medieval English bakers of including an extra loaf when selling a dozen, in order to avoid the harsh punishments for selling short weight. It's comparable to the application of the current-day euro 'e'. This little understood symbol, found next to the weight on commercially prepared foods, is a safety valve for producers to indicate that the weight has been taken as an average over a number of units.

Banana bread

This fragrant, gently spiced tea bread is a true pick-me-up – perfect for ravenous children returning from school, or anyone in need of cheering up. Bananas become much sweeter and more deliciously scented as they mature, so make sure the ones you use are well ripened. They will be much easier to mash too.

Serve this tea bread thickly sliced – just as it is or with butter. After a few days, it's best lightly toasted and buttered.

Serves 8–10
250g self-raising flour
Good pinch of sea salt
1½ tsp ground cardamom
100g unsalted butter, cut into
    small pieces
125g light muscovado sugar
100g raisins
2 ripe bananas (about 250g,
    peeled weight)
1 egg, lightly beaten
1 tbsp demerara sugar

Equipment
1 litre loaf tin, approx 20 x 10cm,
    base and long sides lined with
    baking parchment, short ends
    well greased

Preheat the oven to 180°C/Gas mark 4. Sift the flour, salt and ground cardamom into a large mixing bowl. Add the butter and rub in, with your fingertips, until the mixture resembles medium breadcrumbs. Add the muscovado sugar and raisins and mix lightly until well distributed. Make a well in the centre.

In another bowl, mash the bananas to a soft and slightly lumpy purée. Add the egg and blend together, then pour into the well in the dry ingredients. Mix together with a wooden spoon and then beat until the mixture is thoroughly combined and has a soft dropping consistency.

Spoon the mixture into the prepared tin, levelling it out with the back of the spoon. Sprinkle the demerara sugar over the top. Bake for about 45 minutes until well risen and a skewer inserted into the centre comes out clean.

This cake will keep for 5 days in an airtight tin and freezes superbly.

Variations
Replace the raisins with dates or walnuts.

Bara brith

Bara brith or 'speckled bread' is a traditional Welsh tea bread. The vine fruits used in the recipe are first soaked in tea to give a beautifully moist result. In the Irish equivalent, tea brack, there is often a good drop of whiskey added too. It is easy to make, keeps well and, incidentally, doesn't contain any fat. You can serve it as it is, or spread it with butter. It's also lovely with a slice of Cheddar. This recipe has been in my family for years, but I can't resist sometimes making a few changes, such as varying the dried fruits, replacing the tea with apple or orange juice, or adding a tablespoonful of marmalade. And, as it's such a good keeper and freezes well, you'll find it's worth doubling up the quantities to make a couple at a time.

Serves 16

175ml strong, warm tea
225g mixed dried fruit, such as
    sultanas, currants or raisins
Finely grated zest and juice of
    1 unwaxed orange
150g light soft brown sugar
1 egg, lightly beaten
225g self-raising flour
Pinch of sea salt
1 tsp ground mixed spice

Equipment
1 litre loaf tin, approx 20 x 10cm,
    lightly greased, base and long sides
    lined with baking parchment

I usually use the remains of a pot of tea to steep the fruit. Otherwise, infuse a tea bag in 175ml boiling water for 5–10 minutes to create a good strong brew.

Place the dried fruit, orange zest and juice, sugar and tea in a mixing bowl large enough to hold everything. Cover and leave overnight for the fruit to plump up.

When you're ready to make the teabread, preheat the oven to 180°C/Gas mark 4. Add the egg to the fruit mix and stir in. Next, sift the flour, salt and mixed spice together over the mixture. Using a metal spoon, carefully mix together to a soft dough. Spoon into the prepared tin and give it a sharp tap to level the surface.

Bake in the oven for about 1 hour, until the top is golden brown and a skewer inserted into the centre of the tea bread comes out clean. Leave in the tin for 10 minutes before turning out to cool on a wire rack.

Once cold, wrap the tea bread in greaseproof paper, store in an airtight tin and leave to mature for several days before eating. It will keep for 2–3 weeks in the tin.

Malted fruit loaf

Malt, which comes from germinating barley grains, has long been prized for its nutrients and soothing properties. Some take their malt in the form of beer, or even a shot of whisky, but I can assure you it is equally good in this well-loved fruited tea bread. It was an economical, but very flavoursome bake during the war and post-war rationing years and remains so – the nutty-sweet taste of the toasted barley corn concealing the lack of any butter or other fat.

Makes 16–18 slices

For the loaf
100g malt extract
100g golden syrup
100ml milk
75g dried dates, roughly chopped
75g sultanas
125g self-raising wholemeal flour
100g plain flour
½ tsp bicarbonate of soda
Pinch of sea salt
1 egg, lightly beaten

For the glaze
1 tbsp caster sugar
1 tbsp milk

Equipment
1 litre loaf tin, approx 20 x 10cm,
    greased, base and long sides lined
    with baking parchment

Preheat the oven to 180°C/Gas mark 4. Put the malt extract, golden syrup and milk into a medium saucepan. Stir over a gentle heat until the mixture is hot and all the ingredients are well combined. Remove from the heat and add the chopped dates and sultanas. Mix well and set aside to cool.

Meanwhile, sift the flours, bicarbonate of soda and salt into a mixing bowl and make a well in the centre. Pour in the malty fruit mixture and egg. Using a wooden spoon, beat well until the mixture forms a heavy, sticky dough.

Spoon the mixture into the prepared tin, spreading it out evenly with the back of the spoon. Bake in the oven for about 40 minutes, until the loaf is well risen and firm to the touch.

Meanwhile, to prepare the glaze, dissolve the sugar in 1 tbsp water in a small pan over a low heat. Add the milk, bring to the boil and boil for 1 minute.

Brush the glaze over the surface of the cake while it is still hot from the oven. Turn out of the tin and place on a wire rack to cool. Once cold, this cake will keep for 5 days stored in an airtight tin.

'Bird table' bread cake

Much as I love to watch the sparrows feeding in the garden, this dense pudding-cum-cake, based on an old wartime recipe, is a brilliant way to use up the end of a stale old loaf. I like to add a few nourishing seeds to give a little crunch.

Makes 10 big pieces

250g stale bread, sliced and crusts removed (to feed the birds…)

100g raisins

100g currants

1 tbsp linseeds

1 tbsp sunflower seeds

125g soft brown sugar

1–2 tsp ground mixed spice

Finely grated zest of 1 unwaxed lemon or orange

1 apple or firm pear, finely grated with skin on

75ml rapeseed oil, or 75g unsalted butter, melted and cooled

1 egg, lightly beaten

300ml milk

1 tbsp demerara sugar, to finish

Equipment

25 x 20cm baking tin, 6cm deep (or a tin with similar dimensions), lightly greased and base-lined with baking parchment

Cut the bread slices into quarters, place in a large mixing bowl and cover with about 500ml cold water. Leave to soak for an hour or so.

Preheat the oven to 180°C/Gas mark 4. With your hands, squeeze out as much water from the bread as you can. Return the bread pulp to the bowl. Mix in the dried fruit, linseeds, sunflower seeds, sugar, mixed spice, citrus zest and apple or pear.

Mix in the rapeseed oil or butter, followed by the egg and milk. Using a wooden spoon, beat everything together to form a wet, sloppy batter.

Pour into the prepared tin and bake in the oven for 1¼ –1½ hours or until the top is crisp and golden. While still hot, sprinkle the demerara sugar over the top.

Serve as a hot pudding, with custard, or leave in the tin to cool before slicing and serving as a cake. Once cool, it will keep for a couple of days in an airtight tin. For longer keeping, store in the fridge.

Variations

In summertime, replace the apple or pear with a handful of fresh berries or red- or blackcurrants. At other times, an overripe banana, well mashed, can be used as the fresh fruit element.

'Elevenses' lumberjack cake

As its name suggests, this favourite of the burly Canadian woodcutter, is a hearty cake, full of fruity goodness. It's just the thing to keep the wolf from the door when the hunger pangs kick in and lunchtime still seems hours away.

Feeds 8 hungry lumberjacks

For the cake
2 large eating apples (175–200g),
    such as Cox's or Russets
250g chopped dates
1 tsp bicarbonate of soda
125g unsalted butter, cut into small
    pieces and softened
175g light soft brown sugar
1 egg
150g plain flour
Pinch of salt
Pinch of ground cloves

For the topping
75g unsalted butter
75g soft brown sugar (light or dark)
60g desiccated coconut
75ml milk

Equipment
20cm round or 18cm square cake tin,
    lightly greased and base-lined with
    baking parchment

Preheat the oven to 180°C/Gas mark 4. Peel, core and coarsely grate the apples into a bowl. Add the chopped dates and bicarbonate of soda, cover with 250ml boiling water and stir together. Leave until warm.

Meanwhile, in a mixing bowl, beat the butter to a cream, using a wooden spoon or hand-held electric whisk. Add the sugar and continue to beat until light and fluffy. Beat in the egg until well combined. Stir in the apple and date mixture, including the liquid, and mix well. Sift the flour, salt and ground cloves over the mixture and fold in carefully. The mixture will seem quite sloppy, but this is how it should be.

Pour into the prepared tin and bake for about 40 minutes or until quite firm to the touch. While the cake is in the oven, prepare the topping. Place all the ingredients in a small saucepan and stir over a low heat until the butter has melted and the ingredients are well combined.

Take the cake out of the oven and spread the coconut mix over the top. Bake for a further 25–30 minutes until the topping is golden and the cake is cooked through.

Leave the cake in the tin until completely cool before turning out. Lumberjack cake will keep for 3 days in an airtight tin. If you wish to keep it any longer, because of its high moisture content, it will need to be stored in the fridge.

Seasonal fresh fruit cake
(no sugar)

Goodness, no sugar, eggs or baking powder! But this excellent fresh fruit cake is a brilliant way to make use of any type of fresh fruit in season. I've used plums here, but you could replace them with apples and pears, berries or bananas, peaches, nectarines or even pineapple. The fruit can be all one kind or a mixture, depending on what you have to hand. Likewise, the dried fruit and nut element can be varied.

Serves 12–16
500g plums, stones removed, or other fruit (see above)
100g desiccated coconut
150g porridge oats
½ tsp salt
150g dried apricots, roughly chopped into 1cm pieces, or 150g golden sultanas
100g hazelnuts, whole or roughly chopped
200ml sunflower oil
150g plain flour (approx)

Equipment
20 x 25cm baking tin, about 6cm deep (or a tin with similar dimensions), lightly greased and base-lined with baking parchment

Preheat the oven to 180°C/Gas mark 4. Roughly chop the plums or blitz them in a food processor. (If you are using strawberries, raspberries or other soft berries, simply crush with a potato masher. If you are using pears or apples, grate them straight into the mix.)

Put all the ingredients, except the flour, into a large mixing bowl and mix well together; the mixture will be quite sticky. Sift in enough flour to make a light, crumbly dough – you may need a little more than 150g if the fruit is very moist, or less if it's very dry.

Press the mixture into the prepared baking tray, firming it down with the back of a fork. Bake in the oven for 40–50 minutes until firm and lightly golden. Leave in the tin until cool before turning out.

This cake will keep for 4 days stored in an airtight tin in a cool larder.

Vinegar cake

This lovely, light, everyday fruit cake is easy to make, although it does involve some chemistry! Customarily baked when hens were 'off lay', this East Anglian speciality has no eggs. Instead, the cake is aerated and leavened by a mass of tiny carbon dioxide bubbles that erupt when bicarbonate of soda is mixed with vinegar.

Serves 18

250g plain flour
250g wholemeal flour
Good pinch of salt
200g unsalted butter, chilled and cut
    into small pieces
150g light soft brown sugar
250g raisins
250g sultanas
50g mixed peel (optional)
300ml whole milk, plus 1 tbsp
50ml cider vinegar
1 tsp bicarbonate of soda
2 tbsp golden syrup
1 generous tbsp demerara sugar

Equipment
28 x 22cm baking tin, about 6cm deep
(or a small roasting tin with similar
dimensions), lightly greased and
base-lined with baking parchment,
or for a deeper cake, a 23cm round
or 20cm square tin, lightly greased
and base-lined with parchment

Preheat the oven to 170°C/Gas mark 3. Sift both flours and the salt into a large mixing bowl. Add the butter and lightly rub in with your fingertips (or using a food processor) until the mixture resembles fine breadcrumbs. Add the sugar, raisins, sultanas and mixed peel, if using, and lightly mix together until evenly distributed.

Pour 300ml milk into a large mixing jug and add the vinegar. Dissolve the bicarbonate of soda in 1 tbsp milk. Now the fun begins: pour the bicarbonate of soda mix into the milk and vinegar and watch it rapidly froth up to nearly three times its original volume. Tip the foaming milk into the dried fruit mixture and add the golden syrup. Mix with a wooden spoon until thoroughly blended to a soft, lumpy batter.

Spoon into the prepared tin, spreading evenly with the back of the spoon. Lightly sprinkle with demerara sugar and bake for 1¼–1½ hours, until the top is golden and a skewer inserted into the centre comes out clean; allow up to 30 minutes longer for a deeper cake. Leave in the tin for 30 minutes, then remove to a wire rack to cool.

This cake will keep for up to 3 weeks in an airtight tin.

Boil and bait
fisherman's cake

A saucepan and a wooden spoon are the only pieces of equipment you will need to make this scrumptious moist fruit cake. Eaten with a good chunk of farmhouse Cheddar, creamy Caerphilly or crumbly Cheshire, this is an incredibly easy packed lunch, making it the perfect 'bite' for fishermen while waiting for a fish to bite… If you've not got any dried apricots or figs, simply replace these with currants or sultanas, or use a 500g pack of ready-mixed dried fruits to replace all of the dried fruits in the recipe, which makes it very straightforward.

Serves 10–12

125g unsalted butter or 125ml
   sunflower oil or rapeseed oil
125g light soft brown or
   muscovado sugar
1 good tbsp golden syrup or honey
125ml milk
200g raisins
150g dried apricots, each cut into
   5 or 6 pieces

150g dried figs, each cut into
   6 or 8 pieces
2 eggs, lightly beaten
250g self-raising flour

Equipment
18cm deep round or 15–16cm deep
   square tin, lightly greased and
   lined with baking parchment

Put the butter or oil, sugar, syrup or honey, milk and dried fruit into a saucepan with 125ml water. Stir over a gentle heat until the butter has melted and the ingredients are well combined. Simmer for about 15 minutes, until the mixture is slightly thickened and a soft caramel colour, stirring from time to time to prevent it sticking to the base. Remove from the heat and leave to cool for about 30 minutes.

Preheat the oven to 170°C/Gas mark 3. When the mixture is cool, stir in the beaten eggs and sift in the flour. Then, using a wooden spoon, beat together thoroughly until well combined.

Spoon the mixture into the prepared tin, levelling it out with the back of the spoon. Bake in the oven for 60–70 minutes until the top is evenly browned and a skewer inserted into the centre comes out very slightly sticky. Leave the cake in the tin until cold before turning out.

This is a cake that is better left for a few days before eating. It will keep for several weeks stored in an airtight tin.

Cut and come again
(spelt and pear fruit cake)

Despite its lack of glamour (no cherries or exotic fruits), I put this pear cake in the 'cut-and-come-again' category because it's so good, you just can't help but have another slice. Dependable farmhouse cake recipes like this can be found all over the country. Buttermilk, the liquid left after butter-making, is often one of the ingredients – its acidity works with the bicarbonate of soda to make the cake rise.

Makes 15 pieces

500g plain white spelt flour
Pinch of salt
1 tsp bicarbonate of soda
2 tsp ground mixed spice
200g unsalted butter, chilled and cut
   into small pieces
250g soft brown sugar (light or dark)
175g raisins
175g sultanas
150g currants

2 eggs, lightly beaten
1 tbsp treacle or molasses
300ml buttermilk
2–3 firm medium pears (200–250g)

Equipment
23cm square or 25cm round tin,
   lightly greased and lined with
   baking parchment

Preheat the oven to 180°C/Gas mark 4. Sift the flour, salt, bicarbonate of soda and mixed spice into a roomy bowl, making sure they are well mixed. Add the butter and lightly rub in until the mixture resembles fine breadcrumbs. Add the sugar, followed by the dried fruit. Mix well until all the ingredients are evenly distributed.

Now add the eggs and the treacle to the buttermilk and beat until well combined. Pour the buttermilk mix into the dried fruit mixture. Grate in the pears (skins and all), then mix it all together to a soft dropping consistency.

Spoon the mixture into the prepared tin, smoothing the surface with the back of the spoon. Bake for 30 minutes, then reduce the temperature to 170°C/Gas mark 3 and bake for a further 1¼–1½ hours until the top is nutty brown and a skewer inserted in the centre comes out clean. Leave to cool in the tin before turning out.

Wrap the cake in greaseproof paper and store in an airtight tin. It keeps well for up to 3 weeks, but the chances are it won't be around that long!

P.S. If you can't get buttermilk, improvise by adding 1 tbsp vinegar or lemon juice to 300ml milk; leave for 10 minutes before using. Alternatively, use plain yoghurt.

Dundee cake

The Dundee cake proudly bears a wreath of golden almonds, like an insignia, denoting its authority in the fruit cake world. Its origins are linked with the early Scottish marmalade industry. The Keiller family – pioneering and resourceful marmalade-makers – used factory downtime to make this legend of the Scottish tea table. The original recipe used only sultanas and lots of orange peel. These days, commercial recipes seem to favour a rich mix of vine fruits and cherries.

Serves 12

500g sultanas
75ml whisky
250g unsalted butter, cut into small
   pieces and softened
Grated zest of 2 unwaxed oranges
   (use Seville oranges if in season)
250g light soft brown sugar
5 eggs
275g plain flour
Pinch of sea salt

125g ground almonds
2 tbsp Seville orange marmalade or
   50g chopped candied orange peel
50–75g whole blanched almonds
   (see p.32)

Equipment
20cm round tin, lightly greased and
   lined with baking parchment

Preheat the oven to 170°C/Gas mark 3. Bring the sultanas back to life by placing them in an ovenproof dish, pouring over the whisky and covering the dish with foil. Place in a very cool oven – say 130°C /Gas mark ½ – and leave for 30 minutes to allow the whisky to warm and moisten the fruit.

In a mixing bowl, beat the butter and orange zest to a cream. Add the sugar and beat thoroughly until light and creamy. Add the eggs, one at a time, adding 1 tbsp of the flour with each and beating thoroughly before adding the next. Sift the remaining flour and salt over the mixture and fold in, using a metal spoon. Finally fold in the ground almonds, whisky-soaked sultanas and the marmalade or peel.

Spoon the mixture into the prepared tin, spreading it out evenly with the back of the spoon. Lightly place the whole almonds on top of the cake, starting from the outside, and working towards the centre in ever-decreasing circles.

Bake in the oven for about 1½ hours until a skewer inserted in the centre comes out clean. Check after 1 hour and, if the surface is getting too brown, lay a piece of foil over the top. Leave to cool in the tin before removing.

Wrap in greaseproof paper and store in an airtight tin. It will keep for 6 weeks.

The 'Mother' fruit cake

This recipe makes for a jolly good rich fruit cake. Ideal as a classic Christmas cake, it can also be used to make a traditional Simnel cake or a superb wedding cake. The list of ingredients is not set in stone. For instance, if you don't care for glacé cherries, you can replace them with dried cranberries. Dried pears can be swapped for dried apricots or dried pineapple and if, for some reason, you prefer a booze-free cake, you can use fresh orange or apple juice instead of liqueur. Don't fret if you haven't managed to make the cake ahead of time either – it's still lovely when freshly baked.

The chart opposite will enable you to make a cake/cakes to suit most of your requirements. Apart from these sizes, I sometimes like to use a deep 10cm-diameter pork pie tin (this will take about 500g of cake mix) to make a mini cake – perfect topped with toasted marzipan (see p.59) to give as a small festive gift. The recipe method follows overleaf.

Ingredients	18cm round or 15cm square	20cm round or 18cm square	23cm round or 20cm square	25cm round or 23cm square
Currants	150g	225g	300g	375g
Sultanas	150g	225g	300g	375g
Raisins	150g	225g	300g	375g
Dried pears	100g	150g	200g	250g
Glacé cherries	75g	115g	150g	200g
Orange or lemon zest	½	1	1½	2
Brandy, rum or orange liqueur	1 tbsp, plus 1 tbsp to finish	2 tbsp, plus 2 tbsp to finish	3 tbsp, plus 3 tbsp to finish	4 tbsp, plus 4 tbsp to finish
Plain flour	125g	185g	250g	315g
Salt	Small pinch	Pinch	Good pinch	Big pinch
Ground mixed spice	½ tsp	¾ tsp	1 tsp	1¼ tsp
Nutmeg, freshly grated	½ tsp	¾ tsp	1 tsp	1¼ tsp
Ground ginger	Good pinch	2 good pinches	½ tsp	¾ tsp
Soft brown sugar	100g	150g	200g	250g
Unsalted butter, softened	125g	185g	250g	315g
Eggs, lightly beaten	3	4	6	8
Golden syrup or black treacle	½ tbsp	1 tbsp	1 good tbsp	1½ tbsp
Walnuts, chopped	50g	75g	100g	125g
Cooking apple, peeled, cored and finely grated	100g	150g	200g	250g
Approximate baking time	2–2½ hours	2½–3 hours	3–3½ hours	3½–4 hours
Approximate total weight	1.25 kg	2kg	2.75kg	3.5kg

Lightly grease the base and sides of your chosen tin and line with baking parchment. To prevent the outside edges of the cake drying out, tie a double band of brown paper, 3cm deeper than the depth of the tin, around the outside of the tin.

To get the best out of the fruit, put the first seven ingredients in a large ovenproof dish, mix well together and cover the dish with a piece of foil. Place in a very cool oven, about 130°C/Gas mark ½, and leave for about 30 minutes, to allow the fruit to warm and become a little sticky. As you remove the foil, the fruity aroma will give you a whiff of what is to come. Set aside to cool.

Preheat the oven to 145°C/Gas mark 1–2. Sift the flour, salt, mixed spice, nutmeg and ginger into a large mixing bowl, add the sugar and combine well together. Add the butter, three-quarters of the beaten egg and the golden syrup or treacle. Using either a hand-held electric whisk or a free-standing electric mixer, beat for about 1½ minutes until the mixture is light and creamy. Add the remaining egg and beat for a further 30 seconds.

Add the dried fruit, walnuts and grated apple. Use a large metal spoon to fold them in until everything is thoroughly mixed together.

Spoon the mixture into the prepared tin, smoothing it out lightly with the back of the spoon. Make a slight hollow in the centre of the cake – this will prevent the cake from rising in the centre. Place a piece of foil, with a hole (about 4cm wide) cut in the middle, over the cake tin.

Bake in the oven for roughly half the allotted cooking time. Remove the foil and continue to bake until the cake is golden in colour and a skewer inserted in the centre comes out clean. Trickle the remaining brandy over the top of the hot cake.

Allow to cool completely before turning out. Leave the baking parchment on the cake until you're ready to slice it.

The cake will mature nicely if kept wrapped in greaseproof paper in an airtight container. You can store it like this for up to 3 months.

Variation

Mojita Replace the brandy with rum, the orange zest with lime, the dried pears with dried pineapple and the walnuts with cashews.

Family 'hun-ger' cake

A marvellous family filler, this 1950s recipe for a lightly gingered, not-too-sweet cake came from my friend Juliet, who remembers her mother making it as a beach and picnic cake. Assembled from everyday store-cupboard ingredients, its name is a play on two of the main ingredients – honey and ginger. It is very easy to put together, keeps well and is surprisingly moreish.

Feeds 12 hungry mouths
250g plain flour
1½ tsp bicarbonate of soda
½ tsp salt
1 tsp ground cinnamon
2 tsp ground ginger
Good pinch of ground cloves
125g unsalted butter, softened
125g light soft brown sugar
100–125g runny honey (or set honey, warmed sufficiently to trickle)
1 egg, lightly beaten
150ml plain yoghurt

Equipment
20cm square tin, or a 15 x 25cm baking tin (or a tin with similar dimensions), lightly greased and base-lined with baking parchment

Preheat the oven to 180°C/Gas mark 4. Sift the first 6 ingredients together into a bowl. Make sure they are evenly blended together by either mixing with a spoon or beating with an electric mixer for about 30 seconds on the lowest speed.

Put the butter, sugar and honey into another mixing bowl. Beat thoroughly until well blended and creamy. (It will not be as light and fluffy as a pure butter-and-sugar mix because of the honey.)

Add the egg and 1 tbsp of the flour mixture. Beat thoroughly until the mixture is well combined and like a soft cream. Stir in the yoghurt. Now use a large metal spoon to fold in the dry ingredients, a third at a time.

Spoon the mixture into the prepared tin, spreading it out evenly with the back of the spoon. Bake in the centre of the oven for about 40 minutes until the cake is golden brown and springs back into shape when lightly touched with a finger. Leave in the tin for 20 minutes before turning out onto a wire rack to cool.

'Hun-ger' cake keeps well for a couple of weeks wrapped in greaseproof paper and stored in an airtight tin.

Grasmere gingerbread

This is more a chewy, gingery shortbread than the dark gooey cake we think of as gingerbread. A Lake District speciality, it has been made and sold in Grasmere since the mid-nineteenth century. The original recipe is a well-kept secret. I'm sure it didn't include lime or root ginger, or have almonds on top, but as I've yet to find two recipes the same, I've no qualms about presenting my own take on it. Jolly good it is too – the fruitiness of the lime balancing the fiery bite of the ginger.

Makes 12–16 pieces
125g plain flour
2 tsp ground ginger
½ tsp baking powder
125g fine or medium oatmeal
125g soft brown sugar
175g unsalted butter
50g fresh root ginger, grated, or
    50g glacé ginger, finely chopped
Finely grated zest and juice of 1 lime
2 tbsp flaked almonds

Equipment
20 x 25cm shallow baking tin (or
    a tin with similar dimensions),
    lightly greased and base-lined
    with baking parchment

Preheat the oven to 180°C/Gas mark 4. Sift the flour, ground ginger and baking powder together into a mixing bowl. Add the oatmeal and sugar and mix well.

Put the butter into a small saucepan and heat gently until completely melted. Pour into the dry ingredients, then add the ginger and the lime zest and juice. Using a wooden spoon, pound until the mixture forms a moist dough.

Press the mixture into the prepared tin. It may seem a bit skimpy, but don't worry, this is how it's meant to be – it will swell up in the oven. Sprinkle the flaked almonds over the surface and bake for about 30 minutes until slightly risen and lightly brown. Immediately mark into squares or fingers, then leave to cool in the tin.

Once cold, wrap the gingerbread in greaseproof paper and store in an airtight tin for up to 2 weeks.

P.S. Rum butter, another Lakeland speciality, is rather nice with this gingerbread. To make it, beat together 150g softened unsalted butter and 150g soft brown sugar (light or dark) until light and creamy. Gradually add 50ml dark rum, or to taste – do this slowly or the alcohol will 'split' the mixture and it will curdle. Rum butter is also great served with festive mince pies and Christmas pud.

Gillian's sticky gingerbread

Few things give me more pleasure than sitting in the corner of a cosy café with a cup of coffee and a slice of good cake. That's how I came across this gingerbread, at The Ceilidh Place in Ullapool. It's a deliciously moist, gingery creation, subtly flavoured with lemon zest, which nicely balances the rich sweetness of the cake.

Serves 10

For the gingerbread
100g golden syrup
100g black treacle
75g unsalted butter
75g light soft brown or muscovado
    sugar
150g plain flour
1 tsp ground ginger
½ tsp ground mixed spice
½ tsp ground cinnamon
1 egg, lightly beaten
75ml milk
Finely grated zest of 1 unwaxed lemon

½ tsp bicarbonate of soda
75–100g finely chopped preserved
    stem ginger in syrup (drained)

To finish (optional)
50g icing sugar, sifted
1 tbsp lemon juice or water
50g whole stem ginger (2 pieces)

Equipment
1 litre loaf tin, approx 20 x 10cm,
    lightly greased, base and long sides
    lined with baking parchment

Preheat the oven to 170°C/Gas mark 3. Put the golden syrup, treacle, butter and sugar into a small saucepan. Place over a gentle heat and stir until the butter has melted and the ingredients are evenly blended. Set aside to cool.

Sift the flour, ground ginger, mixed spice and cinnamon into a medium mixing bowl. Make a well in the centre and add the cooled treacle mixture, egg, milk and lemon zest. Using a wooden spoon, beat well until the mixture is smooth and glossy. Dissolve the bicarbonate of soda in 1 tbsp hot water. Add to the mixture with the chopped ginger and mix thoroughly to create a soft, pourable batter.

Pour into the prepared tin and bake in the oven for 50–60 minutes, or until the cake is firm to the touch and a skewer inserted into the centre comes out clean. Leave in the tin for 10 minutes before turning the cake out onto a wire rack to cool.

When cold, if you wish, mix the icing sugar with the lemon juice or water and drizzle over the cake, then top with slivers of stem ginger.

This cake is best stored for 3–4 days before eating. It keeps well for 2 weeks and freezes beautifully.

Bonfire night parkin

A member of the gingerbread family, this treacly oatmeal cake is a speciality of Northern England, Yorkshire in particular. Inextricably linked with bonfire night, it is frequently enjoyed around a blazing fire with a burning effigy of Guy Fawkes, the Yorkshire traitor, on the top. Parkin improves with keeping and is best made ahead of time and left to mature for a couple of weeks. For a change, and to really set things on fire, pep up with a little finely chopped fresh chilli (see variation).

Makes 12 pieces

225g plain flour
3 tsp ground ginger
1 tsp freshly grated nutmeg
½ tsp bicarbonate of soda
Pinch of salt
125g medium oatmeal
Finely grated zest of 1 unwaxed orange
125g unsalted butter
125g light muscovado sugar

100g golden syrup
100g treacle or molasses
75ml milk
1 egg, beaten

Equipment
20cm square cake tin, base and sides
    greased and lined with
    baking parchment

Preheat the oven to 180°C/Gas mark 4. Sift the flour, ginger, nutmeg, bicarbonate of soda and salt into a large bowl. Stir in the oatmeal and orange zest.

Put the butter, sugar, golden syrup, treacle or molasses, and milk into a saucepan. Heat gently, stirring from time to time, until the butter has melted and the sugar dissolved. Remove from the heat and allow to cool before adding the beaten egg.

Make a well in the centre of the dry ingredients and pour in the buttery syrup mix. Blend together until the mixture is glossy and pourable. Pour into the prepared tin, making sure you've scraped all the gooey mix from the sides of the bowl. Give the tin a shake to make sure the mixture is evenly spread.

Cover with foil and bake in the oven for 35–40 minutes. Remove the foil and bake for a further 20 minutes until the cake is smooth and glossy on top and a skewer inserted in the middle comes out clean. Leave to cool in the tin.

When cool, turn out, wrap in greaseproof paper and store in an airtight tin. Leave to mature for at least a week before eating if possible. It will keep for 4 weeks.

Variation
For fiery hot parkin, add 1–2 tsp finely chopped fresh chilli.

Party Cakes

Place a candle on any cake and you turn it into a cake to party with. A simple gesture, perhaps, but more often than not, that's what the archetypal party cake is all about: an effortless centrepiece, adorned with lit candles, enthusiastically presented and accompanied by a chorus of the proverbial 'Happy Birthday to you'. This somewhat *laissez-faire* approach allows you the freedom to choose the sort of cake to make or, perhaps more importantly, the type of cake the recipient truly likes. It needn't be elaborate in ingredients or decorations – a light fruity cake, a simple sponge or even a plate of muffins will do to celebrate the special event.

This aside, there are festivities where a certain type of cake has become associated with the occasion: a rich fruit cake, enrobed in soft, sweet marzipan and crisp royal icing is the classic for the merry Christmas season; it is also the foundation for the Easter Simnel cake and a traditional tiered wedding cake.

When it comes to birthday cakes for children, keep things easy: a glacé-iced jam-filled sponge or a chocolate sponge topped with chocolate icing will always please. The most important thing is that you have the right number of candles on the cake. In all probability, young children will be more interested in blowing out the candles than eating the cake, so expect to re-light them several times. Of course, for girls you can pretty the cake up with fresh flowers or ribbons; for boys, you could create a farmyard scene with model animals, or a football pitch with toy figures.

As time goes by, and your baking skills blossom, I hope you will create all sorts of cakes to celebrate special times and events throughout the year. 'What a swell party this is,' sang Frank Sinatra and Bing Crosby in Cole Porter's *High Society*. Remember, no party is complete without its centrepiece – the quintessential and wonderful cake.

Vanilla cheesecake

Although perhaps considered more a dessert than a teatime cake, the baked cheesecake deserves a place amongst the great cakes of the world. I love to load my cheesecake with plenty of sweet aromatic vanilla, making it a perfect base to serve with fresh seasonal fruit or a thick fruity coulis. Use a young, soft cheese – curd cheese, such as Quark, or a simple cream cheese, but not cottage cheese.

Serves 12

For the base
30g unsalted butter
1 tbsp honey
200g digestive biscuits

For the cake
500g curd cheese or cream cheese
275ml soured cream
1–2 vanilla pods, seeds scraped out,
    or 2–3 tsp vanilla paste or extract
3 eggs, plus 1 egg yolk
175g caster sugar
30g cornflour, sifted

To finish
3–4 tbsp soured cream, plain yoghurt
    or fromage frais
250g fresh strawberries, raspberries
    or blueberries

Equipment
23cm springform cake tin, sides
    well greased and base-lined
    with baking parchment

Preheat the oven to 180°C/Gas mark 4. To make the base, put the butter and honey into a small saucepan and place over a gentle heat until the butter has melted. Stir to combine. Meanwhile, crush the biscuits by either placing them in a large plastic bag and whacking them with a rolling pin, or whizzing them in a food processor to crumbs. Mix with the butter and honey until evenly combined.

Press the crumb mixture into the prepared tin. Bake in the oven for 10 minutes, then remove. Turn the oven setting down to 170°C/Gas mark 3.

In a large mixing bowl, mix the soft cheese, soured cream, and vanilla seeds, paste or extract until well combined. In another large bowl, beat the eggs, egg yolk and sugar together using a hand-held electric whisk or balloon whisk, until fairly thick and creamy. Carefully fold into the cheese mixture with the cornflour.

Pour the cheesecake mix on top of the biscuit base and give the tin a gentle shake to level it. Bake for about 1 hour until it is lightly golden and feels firm when gently touched – the centre may still be a little soft but this will firm up as it cools down.

Remove from the oven and run a palette knife or spatula around the inside edge of the cake tin – this will help to prevent the top splitting as it cools down. Leave the cheesecake in the tin until cold.

To serve, carefully remove the cheesecake from the tin and place on a plate. Spread the soured cream, yoghurt or fromage frais on the top and cover with berries.

This cheesecake improves after a day, keeps for up to 5 days in the fridge and freezes (without the topping and fruit) beautifully.

Mocha cake

This deliciously rich, moist cake, adapted from a recipe given to me by my friend Claire Love, will satisfy the most intense chocolate cravings. I love the combination of dark chocolate and coffee, but this recipe works exceedingly well without the coffee, or you can ring the changes by flavouring the mix with a little ground cardamom or very finely chopped chilli or finely grated orange zest instead. For a softer, sweeter approach, replace the plain with milk or semi-sweet chocolate.

Serves 10

200g unsalted butter, cut into small pieces
200g good-quality dark chocolate, broken into small pieces
2 tbsp strong filter coffee, or 1 tbsp instant coffee powder dissolved in 2 tbsp hot water
50g plain flour
50g ground almonds

5 eggs
75g light soft brown sugar
100g caster sugar
1 tbsp sifted cocoa powder, for dusting

Equipment
20cm springform cake tin, lightly greased and lined with baking parchment

Preheat the oven to 180°C/Gas mark 4. Have ready a saucepan of simmering water. Put the butter, chocolate and coffee into a smallish heatproof bowl and set over the pan, making sure the base is not touching the water. Leave until melted, but don't let the mixture get too hot. Remove from the heat and stir until well combined.

Meanwhile, sift the flour into a bowl and mix in the ground almonds; set aside.

Separate the eggs into two large bowls. Add the brown sugar to the egg yolks and beat, using a hand-held electric whisk, until thoroughly combined and creamy. Now carefully fold in the melted chocolate mix, making sure it is evenly combined – the chocolate has a tendency to sink to the bottom of the bowl, so dig down deep.

Whisk the egg whites and caster sugar together to soft peaks. Carefully fold the flour and almond mix into the chocolate mixture, followed by the egg whites and sugar.

Pour into the prepared tin and bake for about 40–45 minutes or until a skewer inserted in the middle comes out a little sticky. The aim is to slightly undercook the cake so it will be soft and a little sunken in the middle. Leave to cool in the tin.

Before serving, remove from the tin and dust with the cocoa. The cake is lovely eaten warm with a little cream. It will keep for 5 days in an airtight tin in a cool place.

Simnel cakelets

These little Easter cakes are inspired by Kerri Spong, an outstanding cake-maker from Axminster who supplies the River Cottage Canteen and stores with them at Easter. They make a lovely change from the classic marzipan-topped Simnel cake, and they're quick to bake, fun to decorate and scrumptious to eat. You can use ready-mixed dried fruit or mix up a medley of your choice.

Don't just make these little sweet treats for Easter; they adapt brilliantly to other festive occasions. And of course you can soak the fruit in something a little stronger than orange juice if you like!

Makes 12

250g mixed dried fruit
Finely grated zest and juice of
    1 large unwaxed orange
250g self-raising flour
1 tsp ground mixed spice
½ tsp freshly grated nutmeg
175g caster sugar
175g unsalted butter, cut into small
    pieces and softened
3 eggs
75ml milk

To fill and decorate

300g Marzipan (see p.58) (or
    150g if decorating the cakes with
    chocolate eggs)
250g Glacé icing (see p.55)
Chocolate eggs (optional)

Equipment

12-hole muffin tray, holes about
    6.5cm in diameter and 2cm deep,
    lined with paper muffin cases
Small (5–6cm) rabbit, chick or flower
    biscuit cutters (if decorating with
    marzipan shapes)

Put the dried fruit into a bowl with the orange zest and juice. Leave in a warm place for an hour or so to allow the fruit to plump up.

When ready to bake, preheat the oven to 180°C/Gas mark 4. Sift the flour, mixed spice and nutmeg into a large mixing bowl. Add the caster sugar and mix together.

Add the butter, eggs and milk to the flour and spice mixture. Using a hand-held electric whisk, beat for 1½–2 minutes until light and fluffy. Fold in the fruit and any residual orange juice.

Half fill the muffin cases with the mixture. Take 150g of the marzipan and divide it into 12 pieces. Flatten each piece into a disc and place on top of the mixture in the muffin cases. Spoon the remaining mixture over the top of the marzipan.

Bake in the oven for about 25 minutes until the cakes are nicely golden and spring back into shape when lightly pressed. Leave in the tray for about 10 minutes before moving to a wire rack to cool.

Meanwhile, roll out the remaining marzipan, if using, and cut it into Easter shapes with the biscuit cutters. Have the glacé icing ready.

When the cakes are completely cold, top with the glacé icing. Place either a marzipan shape or 2–3 chocolate eggs on top of each one to decorate.

These cakes can be stored in a single layer in an airtight tin for up to a week.

Variation

Christmas cakelets Top with marzipan holly leaves, stars and Christmas trees.

Hallowe'en pumpkin cake

The old Irish custom of making vegetable lanterns to ward off evil spirits has long been associated with Hallowe'en. Irish immigrants in America found pumpkins much easier to carve than the turnips and swedes of their homeland, and so the pumpkin lantern has become an enduring symbol of modern-day Hallowe'en. The carved-out pumpkin flesh is often used to make soup or sweet pies. This cake is another alternative: sweetly perfumed, light and crispy in texture, it's a wicked way to make sure nothing goes to waste.

Serves 12

150g unsalted butter, cut into small pieces and softened
300g caster sugar
3 eggs
340g self-raising flour
225g finely grated raw pumpkin flesh
150g amaretti or dry macaroons, lightly crushed
50ml whole or semi-skimmed milk

To finish (optional)
Orange Glacé icing (see p.55)
Hallowe'en sweets

Equipment
23cm garland or ring mould, well greased, or a 20cm round tin lightly greased and base-lined with baking parchment

Preheat the oven to 180°C/Gas mark 4. In a mixing bowl, beat the butter to a cream, using a wooden spoon or a hand-held electric whisk. Add the sugar and continue to beat until well creamed. (It won't be as light and fluffy as a classic sponge mix.)

Add the eggs, one at a time, adding 1 tbsp of the flour with each, and beating well before adding the next. Sift in half the remaining flour, then use a large metal spoon to carefully fold it in. Repeat with the other half. Fold in the grated pumpkin, crushed amaretti or macaroons, and the milk – to give a soft dropping consistency.

Spoon the mixture into the prepared tin and bake in the oven for 45 minutes, until the cake is lightly golden, springs back to shape when pressed with a finger and is beginning to pull away from the sides of the tin. Leave in the tin for 5 minutes before carefully turning out and placing on a wire rack to cool.

For children, trickle the cake with orange glacé icing and scatter with sweets. For adults, serve it plain with hot mulled cider punch. It will keep in a tin for 5 days.

Variation
Add 50g mini marshmallows along with the amaretti for a gooey Hallowe'en cake.

Hedgelog
(Yule log)

This cake is a nod to the pagan ritual of burning a Yule log at the winter solstice, a ceremony intended to drive away the short dark days of winter. The tradition of making a chocolate log for the festive season originates from the practice. I can assure you I'm not in the habit of burning hedgehogs but, for fun, I have traded in the customary Yule log for this bright-eyed chocolatey 'Hedgelog'.

Serves 10

For the log
150g dark chocolate, broken into
   small pieces
4 eggs, separated
150g caster sugar
1 tbsp icing sugar mixed with 1 tsp
   cocoa powder, for dusting

For the filling and topping
200g tin sweetened chestnut purée
1 quantity whipped-up Chocolate
   ganache (see p.65)

To decorate
Large chocolate buttons
2 hazelnuts
1 glacé cherry

Equipment
20 x 35cm (approx) Swiss roll tin,
   sides greased and base-lined with
   baking parchment

Preheat the oven to 180°C/Gas mark 4. Have ready a small saucepan of simmering water. Put the chocolate into a small heatproof bowl that will sit snugly on the pan without the base touching the water. Set the bowl over the pan and leave until the chocolate has melted, making sure it doesn't get too hot. Remove from the heat and set aside.

Meanwhile, place the egg yolks and sugar in a mixing bowl and beat, using a hand-held electric whisk, for 5–6 minutes, until the mixture is pale lemon in colour. In another bowl, and using clean beaters, whip the eggs whites to firm peaks.

Add the melted chocolate to the beaten yolks and mix until evenly combined. Fold in the whisked egg whites, being careful not to lose too much of the incorporated air.

Spoon the mixture into the prepared tin and bake for 15–20 minutes or until the mixture is firm to the touch. Leave to cool for 5 minutes before covering with a slightly damp tea-towel (to prevent a crust from forming). Leave for several hours.

When ready to assemble, lay a piece of greaseproof paper on your work surface and dust with the icing sugar and cocoa mix. Remove the tea-towel from the cake and invert onto the paper. Remove the tin and baking parchment.

Spread about three-quarters of the chestnut purée onto the cake, leaving a clear margin of about 1.5cm along each edge. Using the paper as a guide, roll up the sponge like a Swiss roll. Place it, seam side down, on a cake board or plate. Shape one end of the cake to create a pointy hedgehog face.

Mix the remaining chestnut purée into the chocolate ganache and smother over the 'hedgelog'. Use the blade of a knife or a fork to prickle up the surface. Insert chocolate buttons for hedgehog spines, hazelnuts for eyes and the cherry for a shiny nose.

Variation
'Seventies' chocolate roulade Fill with whipped cream and dust with icing sugar.

Raisin and cherry stollen

This traditional sweet German Christmas bread is much simpler to make than it looks, so please don't be alarmed by the length of the recipe. The richness of the dough means you need to allow more time for proving than normal bread; the recipe should take about 4 hours from start to finish. You will find this stollen much nicer than the shop-bought alternatives and it doesn't need to be made at the last minute. In fact, it is best made well ahead to allow the marzipan time to relax into the fruit-packed dough.

Makes 2 loaves (18 slices each)

For the dough
200g raisins
100g glacé cherries, quartered
Finely grated zest of 1 large
    unwaxed orange
50ml dark rum
100g unsalted butter
175ml milk
3 tsp (15g) dried yeast
125g caster sugar
500g strong white bread flour
½ tsp salt
2 eggs, beaten
A little sunflower oil, for greasing
50g flaked almonds
Seeds from 6 cardamom pods, crushed

For the filling
250–300g Marzipan (see p.58)

To finish
25g unsalted butter, melted
Icing sugar for dredging

Equipment
1 floured baking sheet

Place the raisins, glacé cherries, orange zest and rum in a bowl and toss to mix. Cover and leave in a warm place to macerate and allow the raisins to plump up while you make the stollen dough.

Melt the butter in a small pan, then leave to cool down. Warm the milk until tepid (not hot), add the yeast and sugar and stir until dissolved. Set aside until the mixture has started to bubble.

Sift the flour and salt into a large mixing bowl. Make a well in the centre and pour in the yeast mixture, melted butter and beaten eggs. Mix first with a wooden spoon, then with your hands, until the mixture forms a dough that comes away cleanly from the bowl.

(continued overleaf)

Turn the dough out onto a floured surface and knead until it is soft, elastic and no longer sticking to the surface. Alternatively, use a free-standing electric mixer fitted with the dough hook to bring the dough to this stage.

Lightly oil a large bowl, place the dough in it and turn the dough so that it is covered all over with a thin layer of oil. Cover the bowl with cling film and leave in a warm place for 1–2 hours or until the dough has doubled in size.

Turn the dough onto a lightly floured surface and knock back. Flatten the dough with the palm of your hand and sprinkle with half the rum-soaked fruit, flaked almonds and crushed cardamom seeds. Mix in by first folding the dough over the fruit, then lightly kneading until the fruit is evenly distributed. Repeat until all the fruit, plus any residual rum, has been worked in.

Divide the dough into two pieces. Flatten each to a rectangle about 25 x 15cm. Split the marzipan in two and roll each piece into a sausage shape the same length as the dough. Position a marzipan roll along each dough rectangle, slightly off centre. Fold the dough over the marzipan to make two long, loose loaves.

Place the loaves, seam side down, on a floured baking sheet. Cover with a tea-towel and leave in a warm place for 1–1½ hours until doubled in bulk. Meanwhile, preheat the oven to 180°C/Gas mark 4.

Bake the loaves for approximately 25 minutes, until pale golden. Immediately brush the stollen with the melted butter, then transfer to a wire rack to cool.

Once cold, dust freely with icing sugar. Wrap in greaseproof paper and store in an airtight tin for a week or so before eating. This stollen will keep for up to 3 weeks.

Variations

Prune and apricot stollen Replace the raisins with chopped prunes, the glacé cherries with dried apricots, the rum with brandy, and the cardamom with ½ freshly grated nutmeg. Work 100g finely diced dried apricots into the marzipan.

Harlequin stollen Omit the raisins and add 50g chopped angelica, 50g chopped candied citron or lemon peel and an extra 100g glacé cherries instead. Use gin in place of rum. Replace the flaked almonds with chopped toasted hazelnuts and the cardamom with 2 tsp fennel seeds.

Snowy Christmas cake

Despite all good intentions, the decorating of our Christmas cake is usually a hurried affair, entrusted to anyone who is willing to take it on. I asked my daughters Pip and Maddy to do the job some years ago, when they were quite young. They spent days making a small forest of green marzipan Christmas trees, which I imagined would be stuck to the sides of the cake. Instead, the girls stood them upright on top, creating a rather magical three-dimensional snowy scene, a tradition we still keep today. To be able to create this look, the marzipan Christmas trees need to be prepared at least a week ahead to allow them time to dry and firm up enough to stand up.

Use the 'Mother' fruit cake recipe (on p.204) to make your cake. The chart below gives you the quantities of marzipan and royal icing you will need depending on the size of your cake. The recipes and directions for applying these to the cake are on pp.58 and 60 respectively.

I have allowed plenty of marzipan, enough for a 1cm covering with some left over for your Christmas trees, or reindeers, stockings, stars – whatever festive decoration takes your fancy. The marzipan trees are made by cutting out coloured marzipan with a tree-shaped biscuit cutter 5–6cm in length. You could make them smaller, but I wouldn't suggest them being any loftier.

Covering	18cm round or 15cm square	20cm round or 18cm square	23cm round or 20cm square	25cm round or 23cm square
Marzipan (see p.58)	500g	750g	1kg	1.25kg
Royal icing (see p.60)	600g	750g	900g	1kg

P.S. If you prefer not to go the whole hog with the royal icing, you can make a very impressive cake covered with marzipan alone. Follow the instructions to toast a marzipan cake on p.59. Decorated with Christmassy marzipan shapes, this makes a lovely alternative to a fully decked out Christmas cake.

Certosino

Festooned with glacé fruits and nuts, this exquisite honey-sweetened Italian Christmas cake is jam-packed with fragrant and exotic things. This recipe, a little altered, comes from cakeophile Alison Finch's informative *Brief History of the Christmas Cake*. Try replacing the cooking apple with fragrant quince, if you happen to have some (see variation, overleaf). Make this well ahead of time: it is a cake which, like so many of us, improves with keeping.

Serves 24

100g raisins
50ml Marsala or brandy
250g runny honey
100g soft brown sugar
60g unsalted butter
350g plain flour
2 tsp bicarbonate of soda
½ tsp salt
2 tsp ground mixed spice
2 tsp fennel seeds, lightly crushed
250g cooking apples, cored, peeled and finely grated
50g pine nuts
100g almonds, blanched and slivered (see p.32)
100g walnuts, roughly chopped
100g dark chocolate, roughly chopped into 1cm pieces
50g crystallised ginger, finely chopped
100g mixed candied orange and lemon peel, roughly chopped into 1cm pieces

To decorate

About 4 tbsp apricot jam, sieved and warmed
A selection of glacé or crystallised fruits, such as cherries, angelica and pineapple
12–16 walnut halves

Equipment

24cm springform round or 22cm square loose-bottomed tin, lined with baking parchment

Preheat the oven to 170°C/Gas mark 3. Put the raisins and the Marsala or brandy into a small bowl and leave to soak for at least 30 minutes.

Put the honey, brown sugar, butter and 75ml water into a small saucepan and place over a gentle heat. Heat, stirring until the ingredients have softened and are well combined, without allowing it to boil. Set aside. *(continued overleaf)*

Sift the flour, bicarbonate of soda, salt and mixed spice into a large mixing bowl. Toss in the fennel seeds and the grated apple. Next, pour in the warm honey mixture and the soaked raisins and mix to a batter. Stir in the pine nuts, almonds, walnuts, chocolate, crystallised stem ginger and candied peel until evenly mixed.

Spoon the mixture into the prepared tin, spreading it out evenly with the back of the spoon. Bake for about 1¼ hours until just firm and a skewer inserted into the centre comes out clean. Leave in the tin until completely cold. Wrap in greaseproof paper and store in an airtight tin until ready to decorate.

Before serving, brush the top of the cake evenly with half the apricot jam. Arrange the glacé fruits and walnut halves decoratively on the top and brush over the remaining apricot jam. Leave to set before serving.

Stored in an airtight tin, this cake will keep for 10 weeks or even longer.

Variation

Certosino with quince Replace the grated apple with 250g quince purée. To prepare the purée, soften the peeled and cored quince by simmering in a little water, with the juice of ½ lemon added, until tender. Then either push through a sieve or purée in a blender or food processor until smooth. Allow to cool before adding to the cake mixture. A wonderful way to use quince.

King cake

This is my interpretation of the French *Galette des Rois*, a delicious almond-rich cake customarily made for Twelfth Night (6 January), when the three kings are said to have arrived in Bethlehem. Traditionally the cake is served topped with a cardboard crown and a small treasure, such as a cake charm or coin, hidden within it. As the cake is cut, the youngest person sits under the table and calls out the name of the guest who should receive each piece. Whoever finds the charm wears the crown, reigns supreme for the evening and is exempt from the washing up…

Serves 12

15–18 glacé cherries
75g plain flour
150g unsalted butter, softened
200g caster sugar
4 eggs
150g ground almonds
About 2 tbsp milk

To assemble
Cake charm or coin
icing sugar, for dusting
150–200g Marzipan (see p.58)

Equipment
20cm loose-bottomed or springform
   cake tin, lightly greased and
   base-lined with baking parchment

Preheat the oven to 180°C/Gas mark 4. Rinse the sticky sugar syrup off the cherries in a sieve with a little warm water. Dry thoroughly with kitchen paper. Cut the cherries in half and set aside. Sift the flour into a mixing bowl and set aside.

In a mixing bowl, beat the butter with a wooden spoon or hand-held electric whisk until very light and creamy. Add the sugar and beat until light and fluffy. Add the eggs, one at a time, adding 1 tbsp flour with each and beating thoroughly before adding the next. Carefully fold in the remaining flour, using a large metal spoon. Fold in the ground almonds and sufficient milk to give a soft dropping consistency.

Spoon the mixture into the prepared tin, levelling it out with the back of the spoon. Drop the cake charm or coin into the mix.

Dust the work surface with icing sugar and roll out the marzipan to a 5mm thickness. Cut into strips 20cm x 1.5cm. Arrange these in a lattice pattern on top of the cake and lightly balance a cherry half in the centre of each of the lattice squares.

Bake in the oven for about 45 minutes, until a skewer inserted into the centre comes out clean. Leave to cool in the tin before turning out. This cake will keep for 2 weeks stored in an airtight tin.

Useful Things

Directory

Bakeware and cooking equipment

Silverwood
www.alansilverwood.co.uk
0121 454 3571

Lakeland Ltd
www.lakeland.co.uk
01539 488100

Kitchen Craft
www.kitchencraft.co.uk
0121 604 6000

Specialist ingredients

Doves Farm
for specialist and organic flours
www.dovesfarm.co.uk
01488 684880

Marriage's
for fine wheat flour
www.marriagesmillers.co.uk
01245 354455

Sharpham Park
for British spelt flour
www.sharphampark.com
01458 844080

Bia Nua
for gluten-free cake flour
www.bianua.com
01460 298060

Billington's
for unrefined sugar
www.billingtons.co.uk
01733 422696

Steenbergs
for organic and fair-trade spices
and other baking ingredients
www.steenbergs.co.uk
01765 640088

Crazy Jack
for organic dried fruit
www.crazyjack.co.uk
01455 556878

Little Pod
for well-sourced vanilla extract/paste
www.littlepod.co.uk
01395 511243

Cocoa Loco
for organic chocolate
www.cocoaloco.co.uk
01403 865687

Green & Black's
for organic chocolate
www.greenandblacks.com
0800 8401000

The Somerset Cider Brandy Company
for English apple brandy
www.ciderbrandy.co.uk
01460 240782

Cakes, Cookies and Crafts
for cake cases and sugared decorations
www.cakescookiesandcraftsshop.co.uk
0845 61 71 810

Conversion charts

Metric quantities are given in the recipes. Use the following conversions if you prefer to work in imperial measures.

Weight

Metric	Imperial
25g–30g	1oz
50g–60g	2oz
100g–125g	4oz
170g	6oz
200g	7oz
225g	8oz
275g	10oz
340g	12oz
400g	14oz
450g	1lb
500g	1lb 2oz
900g	2lb
1kg	2lb 4oz

Liquid/volume

Metric	Imperial
150ml	5fl oz (¼ pint)
300ml	10fl oz (½ pint)
600ml	20fl oz (1 pint)
1 litre	35fl oz (1¾ pints)

1 tsp (1 teaspoon) = 5ml
1 tbsp (1 tablespoon) = 15ml

What is a gill? This old-fashioned term often crops up in old recipe books and one gill is equivalent to 150ml or ¼ pint.

Liquid volume An average lemon will yield roughly 50ml lemon juice. Citrus fruits juice more easily if rolled by hand on a work surface for 2 or 3 minutes.

Oven temperatures

	°C	°F	Gas mark
Very cool	130	250	½
Very cool	140	275	1
Cool	150	300	2
Warm	160–170	325	3
Moderate	180	350	4
Fairly hot	190–200	375–400	5–6
Hot	210–220	425	7
Very Hot	230–240	450–475	8–9

For fan ovens, set the oven 10–20°C lower than indicated in the recipe.

Acknowledgements

I've always baked cakes, but it was only when John Wright (with three River Cottage handbooks under his belt), rather provokingly threw down the gauntlet and challenged me by saying, '*You can't write only one book in your life*,' that I was driven to thinking I could write a book about cakes. And what a joyful journey it's been, with many a happy hour spent in the kitchen, plus all those cakes to eat – thank you, John.

However, it goes without saying, the creation of this book has been far from me alone, but includes a rather wonderful collection of people who have contributed their professionalism – many have also taken on the vital role of 'honorary cake tasters'.

First of all, immense thanks to Gavin Kingcome – it's been simply brilliant to work with you again, Gavin, and your photography has truly illuminated my recipes. Huge thanks also to Nikki Duffy for her expertise, clear thinking and for ironing out any blunders.

Sincere thanks go to Bloomsbury literary experts Richard Atkinson and Natalie Hunt for their unflagging patience and encouragement. To Will Webb, for his inimitable style in bringing the book together. And to editor Janet Illsley for her warmth and absolute care in setting my mind at rest. Thanks also to Antony Topping for keeping a keen eye on the whole project.

A special thank you to Harcombe Farm hens for their constant supply of freshly laid golden-yolk eggs.

To family and friends who have generously given me tips, and those 'lovely hand-me-down recipes' to share with cake-makers the world over. To husband Hugh and daughters Pip and Maddy for never tiring of having to try *yet* another cake and for their obliging and much welcome kitchen porter skills. And again to Pip and also Trish Bye for valuable help on photo-shoot days.

I would like to thank Rob Love for his insight and commitment towards River Cottage.

And, finally, heartfelt thanks to Hugh FW – to you, Hugh, I owe so much for your boundless enthusiasm and inspiration – none of this could have happened without you.

Index

River Cottage Handbooks

Seasonal, Local, Organic, Wild

FOR FURTHER INFORMATION AND
TO ORDER ONLINE, VISIT
RIVERCOTTAGE.NET